£2.49
49

WOUNDS THAT HEAL

Wounds That Heal

Keith A. Fournier

Servant Publications
Ann Arbor, Michigan

Servant Publications
P.O. Box 8617
Ann Arbor, Michigan 48107

Many of the examples mentioned in *Wounds That Heal* are illustrations drawn from the author's personal life. Many involve the author's immediate family members and members of his family of origin. In the case of the author's personal friends from boyhood, adolescence, and young adulthood, pseudonyms have been used, with the exception of Fr. Philip Bebie, C.P. In the case of all other individuals used in personal examples or illustrations, with the exception of celebrities and biblical characters, the names used are pseudonyms and incidents involving such individuals are rendered as fictional composites, having some basis in fact. Any similarity between such names and characterizations and real people is unintended and purely coincidental.

Scripture texts used in this work, unless otherwise indicated, are taken from *The New Revised Standard Version* of the Bible, copyright © 1989, Division of Christian Education of the National Council of the Churches of Christ in the United States of America, and are used by permission.

Quotes from *Beyond Codependency: And Getting Better All the Time* by Melodie Beattie, copyright © 1989 by Hazelson Foundation, Center City, MN. Reprinted by permission.

Quotes from *The Weight of Glory and Other Addresses* by C.S. Lewis, copyright © 1980 by Collins Fount, an imprint of HarperCollins Publishers Limited, London, England. Reprinted by permission.

Cover design by Gerald L. Gawronski / The Look
92 93 94 95 96 10 9 8 7 6 5 4 3 2 1

Printed in the United States of America

ISBN 0-89283-764-0

Library of Congress Cataloging-in-Publication Data

Fournier, Keith A., 1954–
   Wounds that heal / Keith Fournier.
     p. cm.
  ISBN 0-89283-764-0
  1. Suffering—Religious aspects—Christianity. 2. Twelve-step programs
—Religious aspects—Christianity. 3. Spiritual life—Catholic Church.
4. Catholic Church—Membership. 5. Fournier, Keith A., 1954–
I. Title.
BT732.7K586 1992
248.8'6—dc20   92-27966

ACKNOWLEDGMENTS

NO WORK IS COMPLETE without honoring those who made it possible. First on the list is my faithful friend and partner in marriage and family life, Laurine. Next are our children: Kristen, Keith, Ann, MaryEllen, and Joel.

I am also deeply grateful to Dave Came of Servant Publications for his patience and insights in the editing of this book. Writing a book is perhaps the closest to birthing a child that a man can get. If transition is the most difficult part of labor, this entire book felt like one long transition. It was painful, but Dave's assistance was indispensable.

Finally, without the faithful and encouraging help of my assistant, Debra Kiggins, none of this would have been possible. I am truly grateful.

Contents

AUTHOR'S NOTE

Wounds That Heal is my personal story of suffering and struggle, recovery and renewal. The focus is on my family of origin, the family in which I grew up. As with all books, I hope you will read it with a critical eye, so you can determine for yourself what you think about some of the issues discussed in the pages that follow. You may agree with some things and disagree with others. In the end, I hope that you will find much that is a help to your own life.

If any readers use this book to criticize any individual or group, they will have completely misunderstood my purpose. This is simply a book about my life up to this point and about some of the lessons I have learned along the way. It is not a book about blaming others but about taking responsibility for my own life.

Through the prism of my experience—including reflection on Scripture, Christian tradition, and certain principles in the recovery movement—I attempt to shed some light on the mystery of suffering and its deeper meaning in Christ. Understanding and then embracing that deeper meaning has brought healing into my life. I pray the same will be true for all my readers who carry wounds from a painful past.

Introduction

Wounds That Heal is a book about real life, the gritty stuff of daily life that we all face, even when we have faith. It is a book about a personal faith that leads to transformation and conversion—the kind of faith Jesus elicits in the Gospels. It's not a faith that escapes struggle, difficulty, and pain, but a faith that transforms them. It is a book that dares to grapple with the problems of life that just don't go away, like compulsive behaviors, addictions, and predominant faults.

I use the word "grapple," advisedly, because I certainly don't have all the answers. Many brilliant, holy men and women throughout the ages have tried to find them. I stand on their shoulders. What I do offer is my own personal experience and reflection, my experience of recovery and renewal in Christ. Think of me as simply a beggar telling you where I have found the bread that satisfies my soul.

This is a book about dying as well—its finality and its promise of eternal life. There is the pain of loss, but also the hope of eternal life. I offer no formulas or secrets that will make the reality of death disappear in your life. Rather, I show you how God can transform death making it not an end, but a beginning. In that transformation from death to new life, dread gives way to the virtue of hope. I talk not just of physical death, but of the daily dying that is a part of living by faith.

This is a book that links the inevitability of suffering and struggle with the power of recovery and renewal, showing

God's steadfast purpose and plan, even in the midst of struggle. The Christian life and authentic recovery from woundedness need not be at odds with each other. Rather, they can be complementary. Both can lead to ultimate healing. That is why I draw upon the best in the recovery movement to illumine the journey for us.

Let's be honest. Each of us has been wounded, and God allows it. Why? While I don't have the full picture, I have discovered that wounds themselves can heal. Sometimes they heal over time and eventually go away. But many times God uses them to minister an even more profound healing to our bodies and souls, transforming the inner person. For those with the eyes of faith, the promise is even the transformation of our bodies on the Last Day.

The amazing fact that the very wounds, struggles, and difficulties we so often dread can be agents of healing and transformation is not a new thought. But seeing the connection between the Christian wisdom of the ages on suffering and the value of much in the recovery movement today can lead us to a deeper understanding of this mystery. That is one of the key benefits of this book. I seek to combine what Christians have learned about suffering, especially in the Catholic tradition, with key principles and insights from recovery literature which complement that understanding in our day of dysfunctional family life, compulsions, and addictions.

Wounds That Heal, then, is about the mystery of suffering and struggle which men and women of all generations have encountered. They have either avoided and denied this reality, or embraced its deeper meaning and purpose in Christ. Those who have embraced its deeper purpose have discovered conversion and renewal on the other side of their suffering and struggle.

In so doing, they have joined the ranks of the cloud of witnesses (Heb 12:1) who have gone before us. One among them was my good friend, Fr. Philip Bebie, C.P. Let me share his story—a stirring, poignant one that opened my eyes to the way I denied, tried to control, and even avoided suffering in my life.

Tribute to Fr. Philip

I T WAS A COLD, DARK, DREARY DAY in the dead of winter—a day made for somber reflection, a day that would forever change my life. I had boarded a plane in Pittsburgh, Pennsylvania, with a mission—to see my friend, Fr. Philip Bebie, C.P., before he died. I was gripped with fear, sorrow, hesitation, and yet resolve. This strange mixture of emotions surged through me, betraying my inability to confront death and lack of understanding about the mystery of suffering. But I now know I was in very good company. In fact, I believe a majority of people struggle with the same lack, whether they are openly Christian or not.

I hadn't seen Fr. Philip since college. As a transfer student to the then College of Steubenville,[1] I first met him in an empty dormitory named St. Thomas More. It had been set aside as a spiritual renewal center by the president of the college to help revitalize the campus. Fr. Philip was one of the full-time staff who, at the president's invitation, responded to the challenge of renewal, which called for rededicating the college to Jesus Christ. As a transfer student, I too had responded to that call. At the request of the college's president, Fr. Michael Scanlan, T.O.R., I was involved in building the first student "faith household" in the dormitory. The idea was to invite students to live together in commitment to the Lord and one another within a wing of the dormitory, building a genuine experience of Christian fellowship. We would pray together, recreate together, and forge a deep experience of community. These faith households would become the hallmark of the whole student-life model at the college and significantly lead to its transformation.

A PASTOR, A FRIEND, AND A CONFESSOR

At the time, I was alone, full of zeal, and yet desperately in need of a friend and pastor. Philip became both. He was six feet seven inches tall, a man of great stature and dignity, with a heart of holiness and a tremendous love for God's people. He took me under his fatherly wing and helped me find a place at Steubenville and, even more importantly, a home in the heart of my church.

Philip's spirituality was deeply incarnational. He was as much a Christian in prayer as he was enjoying a *Pink Panther* movie, a penchant we both held in common. I remember well the times we would share the simple, joyful things of life, and he would suddenly erupt into a full belly laugh which quickly proved contagious. He would have made a perfect Santa Claus! God was good to me at this crucial juncture in my life; he gave me a priest, a pastor, a friend, and a confessor all wrapped up in this one marvelous man.

Fr. Philip played an even more significant role in my life, however. After struggling with a vocational crisis, Philip's counsel helped me make my choice for marriage. He then prepared Laurine and me for marriage not only by teaching us his profound understanding of this sacrament as a response to the gospel, but by giving us very practical advice that would stand the test of time.

I'll never forget the night that Philip sat with us during our last preparation session. Looking deeply into our eyes and hearts, he encouraged us, "Don't ever forget to tell one another, 'I love you,' to hold hands, and to hug." We laughed, surprised that he would give such advice to us. After all, we could hardly keep our eyes, or for that matter, our hands off one another. But sage advice it has proved. Five children and many years into marriage it remains practical and profound. But so was Philip.

As my college career unfolded, Philip moved on. A member of the Passionists, a Catholic religious order committed to itinerant preaching, his first love was sharing the gospel. The founder of his religious order, Paul of the Cross, had spent his entire earthly ministry preaching the gospel of grace to anyone who would listen. He was an itinerant preacher in the 1600s with a special devotion to the suffering of Jesus Christ. So it was with Philip; he longed to travel and preach about the cross. I remember during my college years hearing him preach with passion about the cross of Christ and the tremendous love of God the Father in sending his Son for our sake. When he got the chance he would set out and give parish missions throughout the country. But his influence on my life would continue beyond college.

We stayed in touch as best we could over the years. He wanted to motivate me to be a faithful husband and father in Christ and would send me little reminders of God's love. You see, the greatest gift Philip ever gave Laurine and me was to preside at our wedding. We were only one of two couples whom he married during his priestly ministry, and he took great pride in his role in our life.

I will never forget Philip standing in front of Laurine and me as he preached his homily at our wedding. It was as though we were the only two people in the congregation. He looked right into our eyes and told us how holy the call of marriage truly was. He talked of the paramount importance of our faithfulness to each other and of the inevitable struggles that would come our way. He was deeply committed to our marriage covenant.

Philip, a celibate priest, understood the mystery of marriage better than anyone I have ever known. He knew its beauty and its sacrifice. He knew how precious it was to God. That is why he was so honored to forsake it for Christ, and offer it to him as a gift of love. He was married to Christ's bride, his church, and he served her with undying affection. He also had a very special place reserved deep in his heart for Mary, the mother of Jesus. Her faith-filled example gave him great strength.

At critical times in our life together, Philip seemed to appear just for our family. For example, our second child, Keith, was born with severe colic. He literally screamed all day and all night. Nothing could bring him or us relief. Racked with fatigue, my wife and I would cry out to God for help, but we felt deeply abandoned. Medication, suggestions from well-intended friends, and even prayer brought no relief.

I was in law school at the time and the pressure of countless hours of study, coupled with the helplessness we felt for our son, led to a severe crisis. Just at the moment we had given up hope, God sent an angel, Fr. Philip. He understood, he listened, and he comforted us. If that were not enough, he prayed and we experienced a complete miracle.

Touching Keith's head, he interceded, "Father, I ask you to look down with favor on this your child, and in the name of your holy child, Jesus, to work signs and wonders. In a special way, I pray that this baby would reflect the humility of Mary in his life, and I ask that she pray with us for his complete healing." Keith slept that night for the first time, and his colic never returned! Philip was a prayer warrior.

AVOIDING AND DENYING THAT MY FRIEND WAS DYING

Over the years our lives got busier—with my career, more children, and our involvement in lay ministry. Regularly, we would hear about Philip's preaching expeditions. But one day we heard news which shocked us, Philip had cancer. Why? The question that is the most often repeated prayer in human history, kept issuing from my heart. Why, God? Why? Why? Why? Of all people, surely he deserved better. Surely you would treat Philip better. Yet Philip got worse.

I recalled the conversations Philip and I had shared about his belief that God allowed those he loved the most to suffer more. The stories of the great saints and heroes of the faith came to mind. I remembered St. Ignatius of Antioch, an early Christian martyr who had asked the Lord to grind him as wheat for eucharistic bread. I also remembered St. Francis of Assisi who so identified with the Lord in his passion that he was granted the stigmata—the opportunity to bear the wounds of Christ in his own body.

"Sure," I'd say, "I understand," but I didn't. Somehow, deep within me, I thought God took suffering away when people were *really* holy like Philip. Soon my emotional response to any news about Philip was purely defensive. I didn't want to hear about it. I buried myself in denial.

I recalled my Aunt Rose, whose untimely death shocked me at the age of six. I pretended it hadn't really happened. I remembered my best friend's brother in high school, taken by leukemia. But I didn't want to feel the fear, the pain, and the doubt all of this seemed to generate. So I blocked it out of my mind. I simply prayed for Philip's healing and conveniently avoided paying attention to any running accounts on his health. To many reading this book, you will recognize the all-too-familiar pattern of avoidance and denial.

But my efforts were as unsuccessful as our efforts always are at avoiding pain. I finally received word that Philip was dying. I knew I had to see him. I couldn't let him go without sharing one more talk, one more laugh, one more prayer, one more hug. Laurine and I agreed that this was our first priority, so I purchased a plane ticket to Hartford, Connecticut. It was such a quick flight, filled with memories and apprehension.

I grabbed a rental car and drove through the dreary cold outside, while I tried to contain the deep sorrow within. I finally arrived at the huge Passionist Monastery where Fr. Philip was staying in an infirmary. This huge building, which in the 1950s had housed over fifty religious men and even more seminarians, was now only half open with seven occupants, one of whom was Fr. Philip. I parked the car and approached the large glass doors.

Before I could reach for the bell, I saw a note on the door. It read, "Keith, I'm waiting for you on the inside, Fr. Philip." So I entered through an old foyer lined with classic works of religious art and turned into a long, dark corridor. I was afraid and apprehensive, but I longed to hug Fr. Philip and be with him during what I was sure was a very difficult time for him. Little did I know what would happen in the next thirty-six hours. Little did I know that he would minister to me in my own ignorance.

MY FRIEND'S SHARE IN CHRIST'S SUFFERING

Out of the tunnel-like darkness of that corridor, I saw a frail old man in a wheelchair coming toward me. "Hello, I'm Keith Fournier, I'm looking for Fr. Phil," I yelled. No response. He was getting closer now and I figured the old fellow was hard of hearing. So in my insensitivity, I repeated myself more loudly. By then I could see his clear, steel-blue eyes, and I knew. Here before me was an old man with shriveled skin and a severely distended abdomen, but those piercing eyes were Philip's. "Hello, Keith, it's wonderful to see you," he responded.

I followed him to the infirmary where, in his characteristically polite manner, he offered me tea or coffee and the best seat. On the wall were two framed letters which immediately caught my eye. The first was addressed to "His Holiness, Pope John Paul II." As I read the text my heart sank. It was from Philip, offering his suffering to the Lord on behalf of all of his brother priests. The response was from Rome, signed by Vatican staff, accepting the gift as a fragrant aroma pleasing to the Lord.

Before I had even completed my reading, Philip wanted to know all about Laurine, the children, and me, our lay ministry, my law practice.... "Wait," I said, "what about you?"

"Jesus has been good to me" he said. "He has allowed me to share in his suffering."

Suddenly, I was confronted with mystery. I had never really understood all that I had read about the saints, martyrs, and heroes of the faith. Now in front of me was a frail old man whose abdomen was distended, filled with a cancerous growth, whose pain was so intense that he could only sleep for thirty minutes at a time. Here was a man whose days and nights were no longer separate because of the intense pain. Here was a man who could only tolerate small amounts of rice which he prepared on his own hot plate. Here was a man all alone in an infirmary, dying and professing that Jesus had been good to him.

"But never mind about me," he added, "what about you, Keith? You look so good!" For a moment, I was unable to speak. All I could do was look into those deep, piercing eyes filled with the serenity of one who has gazed upon heaven.

As the hours unfolded, I was no longer sure whose eyes they truly were, Philip's or Jesus'. I cried. It would not be the only time I would cry during our time together. Laughter and tears seemed to mingle and flow freely in a stream of consciousness and cathartic cleansing.

I stayed with my friend throughout the night, adjusting to his erratic sleeping pattern and listening. He opened his heart to me and shared much that he had learned during this time of his own passion. All of the confusion that I had brought with me dissipated as I heard him laugh. Though not as loud as it had been during the *Pink Panther* movies we saw together, it was still the full belly laugh I remembered so well from my college days.

He prayed with me repeatedly and reminded me of the words and promises of Jesus. Before long I realized who was really sick. I realized who was really filled with cancer and who was really healthy—who was really ready to spend eternity with his Lord. He spoke poignantly of the mystery of the cross in his own life and how he had discovered that this season of suffering had produced more in his life than all his years of study, ministry, and, all too often, prideful pursuits. Through this gift he was ready now, he said, to go home.

He asked me about a mutual friend who was also a priest. "How is he?" Philip asked. "Well, you know him, he'll never change," I replied. To my utter shock, Fr. Philip lurched forward and stared hard at me. "Don't ever say that," he said, "it's practically heresy, he must change. God will see to it. He wants us all to be like his Son." I will never forget the urgency so obviously present in the heart of Fr. Philip about this and other matters.

All too soon it was time to leave. He heard my confession and pronounced absolution over me, laying his large hands on my head and praying that God's tender fatherly love would always guide me. He then reached behind his wheelchair to a shelf and pulled out a small, golden metal tree with bendable branches and gave it to me. " 'Like trees planted by streams of water, which yield their fruit in its season...' may you be, my friend," he said, referring to Psalm 1:3. "Please pull down a branch each day and pray for me as you do."

After I left that day, I was only able to pull down six branches. Philip went home. The tree still stands on my mantle as a tribute to his courage.

I knew that my life would never be the same after that encounter with one of God's saints. I knew so little of the mysteries of God, but one of his stewards had introduced me to a whole new world. Thank God, I was given more time to learn the meaning of suffering and woundedness, which is what this book is about. I write not as one who knows a great deal, but as a student and a fellow pilgrim. Let me share about another part of my journey.

A year after that visit with Philip, I was at home on a fall Saturday. The colorful foliage drew me outside, and I decided to take an afternoon walk. It was getting rather cold, so I went to the attic to get my blue wool overcoat out of storage. I walked through the woods seemingly alone. Suddenly, I was overwhelmed with a sense of the presence of God's peace. I thought about Philip and how much I missed him. As I reviewed my life and many responsibilities, I realized how much I still needed his counsel. To warm my hands, I reached into my pockets and felt a hole in the lining of one of them. This didn't surprise me. After all, this was an old coat—my favorite. But my fingers went beyond the hole to the inner lining and discovered a folded-up piece of paper. I pulled it out, opened it, and read, "Keith, I'm waiting for you on the inside, Fr. Philip."

SPENDING HEAVEN DOING GOOD ON EARTH

In a very real way, Fr. Philip's role in my life has continued beyond the grave. I know that he is waiting for me on the inside. Perhaps it was an answer to his prayer. He told me frequently how much he longed to be like St. Thérèse of Lisieux, who prayed to "spend her heaven doing good on earth."

The story of Thérèse is not unlike that of Fr. Philip. A young woman in love with Jesus and his church, she gave her life to prayer and sacrifice. Only through an extraordinary grant of permission directly from the Vatican was she able to enter the religious life in her early teens. Her short time behind cloistered walls (she died in her early twenties) was filled with excruciating suffering. She literally wasted away from tuberculosis and died. But as with Fr. Philip, the suffering was used to transform and prepare Thérèse for the longing of her heart, eternal union with her beloved, Jesus. Ironically, in Catholic tradition, this cloistered nun has become the patroness of the missions. Story after story is told of her appearing to missionaries at critical times in their efforts to proclaim the gospel. She indeed seems to be spending her heaven doing good on earth.

I have my own heavenly patron now. My experience with Fr. Philip's life and, even more, with his death, has deeply changed me. It has changed, and continues to change, the way

I view almost everything—life, suffering, pain, struggle, and the mercy of God. Yet I so feared seeing my friend, pastor, and hero suffer that I denied it until the very end. I avoided any conversation about Philip's condition. That's the way it is all too often with struggle, pain, and difficulty. We are unable to embrace them and perceive the hand of God in the midst of them. We deny or seek to control our own reaction or that of others around us. We try to run from the painful truth and live in an illusion of control, usually out of fear of being hurt.

I had to recognize that sin is a raging spiritual cancer and so are unresolved, destructive, and compulsive behavior patterns. But they can be transformed and become vehicles of healing both in my life and yours. That is the wonder and mystery of wounds that heal.

Though Fr. Philip *looked* emaciated, consumed, and broken shortly before he went to meet his beloved, he was, in fact, holy, glorified, and ready. But it took eyes of faith to see the truth about his real condition and my own desperate need for healing. It took the willingness to surrender my will, acknowledge my inadequacy, and walk in inner honesty.

In a strange and mysterious way, pain, struggle, and mistakes are a part of the process that the Lord himself uses to make us more like himself. That is not simply a statement of piety, but a fundamental, liberating truth. My own life, as you will see in the pages of this book, is a testimony to that truth. Though God sometimes intervenes to take away pain and brings immediate healing, our relationship with God in Jesus Christ is not an aspirin. Hurt, pain, failure, struggle, weakness, mistakes, and even compulsive behaviors can become part of his divine plan for each of us.

In fact, if we respond in faith, they become part of a much deeper healing, just as cancer was for Fr. Philip. I will never forget his reply when I asked him how he was. "I am well," he said, "God is good." Philip discovered a mystery I had never understood and am still trying to comprehend completely. Philip wasn't saying that illness is intrinsically good. No, rather God is intrinsically good and wants only our good, even in what seem to be the most difficult and trying circumstances. He will use all that is available to transform us by love, into love.

In the clear, steel-blue eyes of my friend, Christ's priest, I saw the truth of this mystery and I will never be the same. To see the truth and be changed by it, I needed to overcome my own natural response of denial, control, and avoidance. Though I have still not arrived, I have made some progress. I have also encountered continual roadblocks on my journey. More about that in the next chapter.

Yet along the way, at every turn in the road, it has been comforting to know that my friend—my heavenly patron—is waiting for me on the inside, beckoning to me, and showing me his wounds, which are a share in the wounds of Christ. Wounds that heal.

Denial— One of the Games We Play

I didn't do it. Nobody saw me do it.
You can't prove a thing.

—Bart Simpson

I LIKE *THE SIMPSONS.* I know a lot of people don't. In fact, I know a lot of my Christian readers may be scandalized by my forthright expression of appreciation for this popular but controversial animated television program.

When *The Simpsons* first began to air, a lot of people told me that I shouldn't like them. They said that *The Simpsons* only reinforced "everything that's wrong with the family." They reasoned that it not only wasn't a Christian program, but was destructive of traditional family values. Unfortunately, because my Christian friends told me these kinds of things, I decided I didn't like *The Simpsons* either, even though I had never seen an episode. It's funny how that's often typical of our approach to forming opinions about things.

Several years ago I visited my parents in Florida. One of the unusual, or perhaps usual, things about my family is that it is like two families. Though I was for many years the youngest of three children, my parents had a "change-of-life baby." My little brother was born just when I was leaving home in the midst of my teenage rebellion. It presented a fresh opportunity for my parents.

During my stay, he asked me with great eagerness whether I wanted to watch *The Simpsons*. I quickly mouthed what I had picked up from my Christian friends. "No" I proclaimed, "That's a terrible program. It's destructive of family values." Of course, my brother recoiled, confused as he was between admiration for his older brother and appreciation for what I would soon come to discover is a genuinely funny program. Fortunately, he had enough courage to stand up to my narrow-minded bullying. "Oh, come on, Keith, watch it with me," he retorted. And I did. I still can't remember the last time I laughed as loudly at a television program.

What is presented in color animation is a very realistic portrait of many American families, including the dysfunctional ones in which many of us were raised. Like countless fathers, Homer Simpson is hot tempered and has difficulty showing his children affection. Like many mothers, Marge Simpson is always trying to take care of everybody else, but is never quite able to take care of herself and understand the critical connection between the two. Meanwhile, the kids are always at each other's throats. Yet in spite of it all, you know that Homer, Marge, and the kids love each other. In the same way, in spite of everything that went wrong in my family of origin, we always loved each other. Even in the family that I'm raising today, many of my mannerisms and behaviors are more like Homer than like Jesus. And no matter how hard I try, my kids still seem to relish ridiculing one another.

Let's face it. The phenomenon of the so-called "dysfunctional family" is a reality. I grew up in one and perhaps you did too. But all too often denial sets in, and we refuse to admit it.

Take *The Simpsons*. Among the Simpson artifacts in my home is a family portrait of the clan. Homer is yelling, Bart is choking his sister, and Marge is in perfect control. The caption underneath says it all. Homer directs the troops, "Remember, if anyone asks, we're a nice, normal family." Denial—plain and simple, and also humorous to boot. That's *The Simpsons.*

Since that evening I have watched *The Simpsons* regularly. Of course, I try to explain to my children (I have five), that there are things that I don't agree with on many of the episodes. Sometimes I don't think the story line promotes the right values, so we switch channels. But I have learned to laugh about very painful but real things in my life.

I am a compulsive overeater, a problem that stems from the way I was raised. My difficulty in keeping off pounds is very real and has been lifelong. I have learned that gaining weight is a thorn in my side, among others (2 Cor 12:7).

I assure you, though, there is nothing more humbling than a weight control problem. It is one of those compulsive behavior patterns that is impossible to hide, even if you've got the best tailor in town! The fact is when you're fat, it shows.

For instance, I have done two installments of a TV series entitled "Domestic Church" for Mother Angelica's Eternal Word Television Network—a nationwide, Catholic cable network that provides instructional and inspirational programming for Christian families. In the first installment of thirteen programs, I was slim and trim. Less than a year later, when the second installment of thirteen programs was taped I had picked up a considerable amount of weight. You can imagine the interesting letters that I received! Many people seemed to like the second installment better, which was formatted as a talk show. But they liked the slimmer me in the first installment. There was no denying that I had a weight problem. It was there in living color for all to see.

A weight problem is not the only painful reality in my life that has kept me close to the cross and forced me to face myself. As I grow older, I have learned more about my own impatience, curtness, and intolerance in dealing with others. But each of these realities can and does open me up to a deeper understanding of grace—unmerited mercy and favor. I am finally learning to lighten up in my own intense efforts at being perfect and building the perfect Christian family.

But years ago it was different. For two years we, as a family, extended ourselves by bringing in single people to live with us. Part of the idea was to give them a family environment and help prepare them for the vocation of Christian marriage. However, we lived a lifestyle in the home that was too monastic and spartan for family life. Our household schedule ran like precision clockwork.

I remember having guests at our home one day who remarked several weeks later, "It was like living in an army barracks. You got more accomplished by nine o'clock than most people do all day." Though well-intentioned, this sociological experiment was ultimately a failure. It looked good on the outside with its regular prayer time and perfectly ordered approach to chores, but it squeezed the spontaneity, joy, and vitality right out of our family life. The children and Laurine look back at that time now and laugh, but I am only learning now to laugh. After all, we thought at the time we were living the ideal Christian family life.

As you can see, I have resorted to denial many times in my life. I still resort to it. It creeps up all too often unnoticed—like an unwelcome intruder in the middle of the night. And before I know it, it has laid claim to my most treasured possession, my freedom, compromising my integrity. All of this, while very often parading as a welcomed guest. I even denied my dear friend Philip's impending death. Unable to deal with the deep emotional pain his advancing illness caused and the challenge to my own limited spirituality, I simply pretended it wasn't happening. Sound familiar?

Last year at the request of my five-year-old, MaryEllen, I bought a cassette tape of *The Simpsons*. The lead tune on the tape was entitled, "The Bart Man." A week later I came home from a hard day of work at the office. Before I could even eat dinner, I was accosted by two of my three girls. "Please, Dad, watch our dance," they begged. Reluctantly I agreed and nestled down on the living room couch where I could have slept for the entire evening. They brought down their own acceptable version of a "boom box" and popped the tape in. I was treated to a delightful demonstration of contemporary dance choreographed to a rap song by Bart Simpson himself, the hero of the show. The words jumped out of the player as they were repeated over and over again, "I didn't do it. Nobody saw me do it. You can't prove a thing." Denial, plain and simple. Like father like son, Homer would have been proud of Bart!

The song kept coming back to that phrase and the phrase keeps haunting me. It explains one of the greatest impediments to growth in the Christian life and in basic human development—denial.

I have denied responsibility for hurt caused in other people's lives through my misguided approach to leadership. I have denied responsibility for hurt caused in my children's lives by intolerant and insensitive fathering. I have even denied responsibility for the bad fruit produced in my own life by compulsive overeating. I am not afraid to acknowledge these things any longer. In fact, simply acknowledging my responsibility has opened some prison doors. All too often, however, we refuse to accept responsibility for our choices and actions.

THE BAD FRUIT OF DENIAL

Denial is not a new phenomenon. It seems to go hand-in-hand with our fallen human condition. We read in the first book of the Bible, Genesis, of the early history of denial. When Eve, the mother of the human race, succumbed to the temptation of the Serpent to eat of the forbidden fruit, the first thing she did was share her newfound enlightenment and its insidious result with her partner, Adam (Gn 3:6).

What immediately follows is most interesting. It is the first biblical example of denial, but certainly not the last.

Then they heard the sound of the Lord God walking in the garden in the cool of the day, and the man and his wife hid themselves from the presence of the Lord God among the trees of the garden. But the Lord God called to the man and said to him: "Where are you?" And he said, "I heard the sound of thee in the garden, and I was afraid, because I was naked; and so I hid myself." He said, "Who told you that you were naked? Have you eaten of the tree that I commanded you not to eat?" The man said, "The woman whom thou gavest to be with me, she gave me fruit of the tree, and I ate." Gn 3:8-12

It is a slippery phenomenon, this denial we all seem to fall into, time and again. Rather than accepting responsibility for his actions, Adam denies and blames another. But this pattern of denial and blame does not end with Adam. As we read further: "Then the Lord God said to the woman: 'What is this that you have done?' The woman said, 'the serpent tricked me: and I ate'" (Gn 3:13).

This story, among many other things, shows us that the pattern of denial, avoidance, and blame is a typical human response mechanism whenever people are questioned about their behavior and motives. This tendency has been with us from time immemorial. Further on in Genesis, the first child of Adam and Eve commits fratricide. He too, like his father and mother, is confronted by the Lord. Once again, however, we see bald-faced denial. "Cain said to his brother Abel, 'Let us go out to the field.' And when they were in the field Cain rose up against his brother Abel and killed him. Then the Lord said to Cain, 'Where is your brother Abel?' He said, 'I don't know; am I my brother's keeper?'" (Gn 4:8-9).

But not only is the entire history of the human race filled with this kind of denial, if we let down our guard and are honest with ourselves, we will readily admit our personal history is as well. At almost every stage of growth in our lives, we are faced with the choice either to deny wrongdoing, responsibility, and accountability for our actions, or to acknowledge, admit, and, whenever necessary, repent for our actions, so we can move on. "I didn't do it. Nobody saw me do it. You can't prove a thing." It's unsettling, isn't it?

This is why the words of the offspring of Homer Simpson have rung so true for me. The pattern is typically denial, then more denial, and finally a legalistic effort to protect ourselves from any blame. Well, why is it so hard to throw off the yoke of denial?

What we see from Adam, Eve, Cain, and so many other biblical characters is still reflected on our TV screens and in our daily lives. We all too often refuse to accept responsibility for our choices and actions. We deny, avoid, and consequently never reap the fruit of growth and freedom on the other side of admission. Perhaps it's because we fear the consequences of "coming clean."

So we fail to grow up, and thereby mature in holiness. We also find ourselves robbed of happiness as we wander through life subjected to shame and guilt that doesn't come from God, but from ourselves. It is worth noting that after Cain killed his brother he was banished to the land of Nod (Gn 4:16), which means a place of wandering.

As a teenager, under the misguided notion that I was seeking the ultimate truth, I wandered through a myriad of bankrupt spiritualities which roared like wildfire throughout the Boston area. I attended any lecture I could find that offered "the truth"—be it Scientology, Krishna Consciousness, or the Divine Light Mission. I wandered through a sea of pop spiritualities. I wandered as well through a sea of political radicalism.

At only fifteen, I was exposed to the Students for a Democratic Society (SDS). Two young men who had graduated from my high school got caught up in the movement. In fact, they joined its most militant faction, the Weathermen Underground. They invited my friend, Joe, and me to their political collective in Boston, Massachusetts. We sat around a long table with these self-styled "revolutionaries" and heard their analysis of what was wrong with the world. Posters decorated the walls of their apartment with such notable characters as Che Guevara, Mao Tse Tung, and Karl Marx. We even helped them hand out leaflets advertising the "T.D.A." (The Day After) demonstration protesting the 1968 Chicago Democratic Convention. Something about their dedication to changing the world appealed to my own dissatisfaction and rebellion.

This radicalism spurred me to edit the first underground

newspaper in my high school. It was called "Metamorphosis." In retrospect, I see that the name deeply reflected the desire in my soul to be transformed. I also led a march around the flagpole at school to "free Bobby Seale," an imprisoned militant Black Panther party member. Yet none of this political involvement satisfied the deep longings of my heart.[1]

I would later come to realize that the Lord had never left me, yet I had wandered from him. Have you ever felt at times that you have wandered far from the Lord—perhaps locked in a pattern of denial and seeming control of your life?

One of the lessons I think I've learned, but seem to need to learn again and again, is that God is quick to forgive if we but ask and so are many of the people we have hurt. The problem is that we don't take responsibility. We deny, we justify, we simply avoid certain people and situations. We wander, chasing after every fad and fancy to fill the emptiness within.

In the past fifteen years there has been a growing recognition of the impact felt by parents, children, and grandchildren of "dysfunctional" families. Recovery literature talks a lot about denial. In fact, critical to any Twelve-Step process (most of them have been adapted from the Twelve Steps of Alcoholics Anonymous) is the first one of admission. That is the greatest weapon against denial—admitting that we have made a wrong choice and acknowledging our responsibility for it.

That finally began to happen for me on a beach in Santa Cruz, California. After years of wandering in my teens—exhausted, disillusioned, and frightened—I knelt on that beach and reviewed my entire life.

I held in my hands a letter from my friend, David, who had gone to Israel to find his Jewish roots. My parents had forwarded it to me. I opened it up and it began with these words from Psalm 119 (RSV), "How can a young man keep his way pure? By guarding it according to thy word...." David went on to share with me about his acceptance of Jesus as his Messiah. My Jewish friend was telling me about Jesus!

Here I was a Catholic, but I quickly realized as I read through the pages of the letter that David's relationship with Jesus was alive and personal, while mine no longer was. I had to admit that I had left my own roots and had been looking for meaning and truth in all the wrong places.

Those in the recovery movement would say that I had taken the first step of admission, admitting that I had made wrong choices and acknowledging my responsibility for them. That certainly is consistent with Christian morality. Yet many in the Christian community are concerned that the spirituality emerging out of recovery literature represents a threat to the orthodox Christian message.[2] While it may be true that some recovery literature has watered down the notion of sin, I am personally convinced that much of the recovery literature is simply a restatement of the traditional Christian message of conversion for our times. The emphasis is upon a process which continues through one's entire life, not simply a one-time event.

The apostle John in his first letter reminds us of a consistent biblical theme: "If we claim to be without sin, we deceive ourselves and the truth is not in us. If we confess our sins, he is faithful and just and will forgive us our sins and purify us from all unrighteousness. If we claim we have not sinned, we make him out to be a liar and his word has no place in our lives" (1 Jn 1:8-10, NIV).

It seems so simple. Ours is a God of unconditional love and mercy. However, this is a message that we human beings have a very hard time hearing. One of the pioneers of the modern recovery movement, John Bradshaw, talks about "toxic shame." In his words:

> In itself, shame is not bad. Shame is a normal human emotion. In fact, it is necessary to have the feeling of shame if one is to be truly human. Shame is the emotion which gives us permission to be human. Shame tells us of our limits. Shame keeps us in our human boundaries, letting us know we can and will make mistakes, and that we need help. Our shame tells us we are not God. Healthy shame is the psychological foundation of humility. It is the source of spirituality.

What I discovered was that *shame as a healthy human emotion can be transformed into shame as a state of being. As a state of being, shame takes over one's whole identity. To have shame as an identity is to believe that one's being is flawed, that one is defective as a human being. Once shame is transformed into an identity, it becomes toxic and dehumanizing.*[3] **emphasis mine**

Toxic shame, unlike healthy guilt over wrongdoing, is the bad fruit of denial. If we do not acknowledge that we have made wrong choices and have acted in ways that have hurt others and offended God, we will be poisoned by toxic shame. It remains in our systems and plagues us with poor emotional health. It affects our ability to perceive what is really happening in our lives and who we really are in the eyes of God. It eats away at our self-esteem and destroys our awareness of our dignity as God's sons and daughters. Yet many of us spend much of our lives in denial. "I didn't do it. Nobody saw me do it. You can't prove a thing."

CULTIVATING INNER HONESTY

Perhaps we have experienced a wrong notion of the God of the Bible and we have an unhealthy fear of punishment. This tends to happen when we have been raised in a family that is religiously dysfunctional. Even religion itself can become a substance of addiction, misused and abused. We can use religion to hide behind. We can mask our true feelings and identity. We can use it to excuse ourselves from personal responsibility by claiming either that the Lord made us do it or, in some instances, to use the old line from Flip Wilson, "The Devil made me do it."

We can even use religion to banish others who are different from us. Perhaps we have no room for them in our system. We banish them to the world under the mistaken guise of remaining holy ourselves. We can even use religion as a way to pretend we are someone other than our true selves. We can wear one face on Sunday and a different face the rest of the week. This kind of approach to religious faith is toxic in that it poisons rather than nourishes our lives. But true religious faith enhances what we are and helps us to discover what we can become. Some contemporary writers have handled this subject very well recently.[4]

Too many times in religious circles, we place undue emphasis on the appearance of obedience to the detriment of honesty. Which was worse in Eden, the disobedience or the denial? Which was worse with Cain, the disobedience or the denial? Which was worse with Judas, the disobedience or the denial? Though both were bad, denial was worse. The reason is obvious. Without the denial, there could have been recovery, forgiveness, and healing. Of course, sin is offensive. But God is merciful. It is when we hide behind our walls of denial that we miss his mercy.

Remember the story of Peter. He denied the Lord three times, but later he acknowledged his responsibility and sought forgiveness. Not only was he forgiven and restored, he went on to become the rock upon which the Lord built his church (Mt 16:18). Peter overcame his denial and encountered the Lord on the other side of his self-constructed wall of pride and fear of rejection by others.

There is a beautiful hymn of the early church in St. Paul's second letter to his disciple Timothy. "Here are words you may trust: 'If we died with him, we shall live with him; if we endure, we shall reign with him. If we deny him, he will deny us. If we are faithless, he keeps faith, for he cannot deny himself'" (2 Tm 2:11-13, NEB). Peter experienced the truth of these words and so can we. We serve the same God.

A key to overcoming denial is honesty. I'm talking about gut-level inner honesty. Denial is dishonest. Peter wanted to be faithful. At the Last Supper, before his Lord would be led away to be crucified, Peter expressed his heartfelt desire to remain faithful: "Jesus said to them, 'You will all become deserters.'... Peter said to him, 'Even though all become deserters, I will not'" (Mk 14:27a and 29).

But he did fall away and so do we. We fail to recognize Christ in the many ways he manifests himself—in the faces of the homeless, in the voices of the poor and disenfranchised, in the cries of our own children, and in our own failures. Failure, struggle, error, and, unfortunately, sin are a part of our human experience. Peter was more devastated by his own failure than the Lord. Jesus had foreseen it (Mk 14:30). Peter had not.

As a result, Peter went through the Valley of Disillusionment.[5] This phrase refers to seasons in our lives that seem devoid of inspiration and encouragement. These are "dark nights of the soul," as St. John of the Cross called them, or "the desert experience," as many contemporary spiritual writers refer to them.

Peter was going through such a valley. Contrary to the experience on Mount Tabor (Mt 17; Mk 9), where he had witnessed the Lord transfigured before his eyes, Peter was not experiencing glory any longer. Rather, he was experiencing deep regret and remorse. Peter had been comfortable on the Mount of Transfiguration. In fact, he suggested, "Lord, it is good for us to be here; if you wish, I will make three dwellings here, one for you, one for Moses, and one for Elijah" (Mt 17:4).

In that transfiguration experience, Peter was given a glimpse of heavenly glory. He saw Jesus as he will be for all time and Moses and Elijah transfigured by the same Holy Spirit that would raise Jesus from the dead.

Of course, Peter was comfortable in that glory. He wanted to bask in it. So it is often with us, isn't it? We love the times when we experience the power and presence of God—when things are going well. However, much of life is lived in the valleys rather than on the mountaintops.

It is important to remember that this denial, though painful and disillusioning, became the very material out of which Jesus was able to fashion Peter into the solid rock he would later become. In fact, in a very real sense, Jesus was there in the midst of denial: "About an hour later still another kept insisting, 'Surely this man [Peter] also was with him; for he is a Galilean.' But Peter said, 'Man, I do not know what you are talking about!' At that moment, while he was still speaking, the cock crowed. *The Lord turned and looked at Peter.* Then Peter remembered the word of the Lord, how he had said to him: 'Before the cock crows today you will deny me three times.' And he went out and wept bitterly" (Lk 22:59-62, emphasis mine).

Can't you picture the scene? The Lord looked straight at Peter—eyeball to eyeball. He does the same to us. He is well aware of our propensity toward denial. But as he did with Peter, he wants us to face our own failures, mistakes, shortcomings, and sin. We don't. We want to hide them. To pretend they didn't happen. "I didn't do it. Nobody saw me do it. You can't prove a thing." That is what denial is all about. It is probably the most powerful thing that holds us in chains.

Peter's disillusionment was not a cause for ultimate regret. Rather, it was used as clay in the hands of the divine potter. After all, the word literally means, "to be free from an illusion." We all too often live our lives in illusion and not reality. There is nothing like failure to strip away the facade of our own pride and self-satisfaction. Disillusionment became a means to real inner honesty for Peter, just as it became a means to inner honesty for me on that beach in California.

Not only was Jesus looking straight at Peter in the midst of his denial, but he wasn't the least bit shocked by it. He knew it was going to happen, he foresaw it, and even warned Peter about it. But he also knew that it was a critical juncture in Peter's life. It was Peter himself who was shocked. Funny isn't it, so it is with us. We have those times when we have failed, and we cannot believe we have done it. Rather than acknowledge, admit, and find freedom and forgiveness from the Lord, we avoid, hide, and deny it at all costs.

The Lord knows what we are made of, just as he knew what Peter was made of. Yet he chose Peter and he chooses us. Weak, as we are, he desires that his power be manifested through us to a needy world (1 Cor 1:27). Yet we find that so hard to believe, don't we? We also find it hard to believe that others love us "warts and all." All too often we fear close relationships, most particularly one with God. All too often, sometimes unknowingly, we sabotage our relationships.

Not only was Jesus aware of Peter's denial, not only did he love him in the midst of it, but he walked with him through it. "Simon, Simon, listen! Satan has demanded to sift all of you like wheat, but I have prayed for you that your own faith may not fail" (Lk 22:31-32a).

Jesus interceded for the protection of Peter's faith. In fact, he prayed that Peter would be used to strengthen his brothers (Lk 22:32). That prayer, like all of the prayers of the Son of God, was answered in spades. That same Jesus prays for us at the right hand of the Father. He uses failure, struggle, and pain, as he did for Peter, and as he has done for so many others throughout the ages, to teach us of his love.

Peter gives me great hope. He is a wonderful example of what it means to be fully human and fully in love with the Lord. He was nearby at most of the significant moments in Jesus' ministry. Yet on most occasions he responded in ways that were less than heroic. He was afraid to walk on the water; he doubted the miracle of the loaves and the fishes; he tried to take control at the transfiguration; he fell asleep in the garden; he denied Christ; he deserted Jesus at the cross. He even, at least initially, denied his own weakness, frailty, and failures.

Yet though he was impetuous and stubborn and proud, he was also decisive, wholehearted, sincere, and ultimately faithful. He didn't run away when all was said and done. He didn't give up hope. He didn't run from the Lord when the risen Lord appeared and looked him straight in the eye. He threw off the yoke of denial and acknowledged his powerlessness and lack of control. He owned up to his failures. So the man who denied the Lord was used by the Lord in marvelous ways. Just read the first part of the Acts of the Apostles. Humiliated by his own failure, he became even more valuable to the kingdom.

This man in the Acts of the Apostles was not the Peter *before Calvary*, but the Peter afterward. This was the Peter who had journeyed through the Valley of Disillusionment, the Peter who had given up confidence in himself alone, the Peter who had been reinstated by Christ and then had preached to the multitudes on Pentecost in Jerusalem. This was the man who had been changed and purified through the fires of struggle, denial, and sin to lead the church. He had discovered true spirituality. So must we. We are always desperately in need of the God of grace. The New English Bible translates the words of Jesus in Matthew 5:3: "How blest are those who know their need of God; for the kingdom of heaven is theirs" (NEB).

In the Easter Vigil Liturgy of the Roman Catholic Church, there is a marvelous proclamation: "Oh happy fault, oh necessary sin of Adam, that won for us so great a Redeemer." The reference is to the fall. Strange, isn't it? Unless seen in the context of the broader revelation of grace. It is failure, struggle, pain, and sin which can become the very wounds that heal. The choice is ours, to deny or to acknowledge them.

The Grand Illusion of Control

As of now, I am in control here, in the White House.[1] Secretary of State, Alexander Haig
March 30, 1981

I REMEMBER VIVIDLY that fateful day in 1981 when the nation stood still. For me, and countless others of my generation, the news was all too reminiscent of past national traumas: the assassination of John Kennedy, Robert Kennedy, Martin Luther King, Jr.,... and the list goes on. President Ronald Reagan had been shot. Like so many others I looked for hopeful news, direction, or at least information. Then Secretary of State Haig came on the television and uttered those astounding words... "I am in control here." Was he? Of course not. In fact, his action would later bring about the virtual end of his political career.

In his insightful account of the Reagan years, Martin Anderson recounts:

> We all knew what Haig was doing. Had he announced that he wanted to address the nation from the press room, he would have been overruled. Had he ordered anyone in the

room to do anything, he would have been politely ignored. He wasn't in control of anything.

The man who was in control, Ronald Reagan, was temporarily indisposed....

Haig's quaint notion that he was in control was a *fantasy existing only in his mind.* But he probably knew that, too, perhaps even better than anyone in the room. What he saw, and seized, was an opportunity... to talk to millions and millions of people and to give them the impression that he was in charge."[2] **emphasis mine**

I have always been struck by then Secretary of State Haig's words and actions. Somehow I think they keenly demonstrate both the subtlety and illusion of control in all of our lives. He wasn't in control of the White House or the nation. In fact, he was relatively low on the totem pole of succession to the presidency in the event of an assassination. If anyone had addressed the nation after President Reagan was shot, it should have been then Vice President George Bush. Secretary of State Haig was deluded and the impression he sought to convey was not real, but misleading and confusing to many. My own immediate reaction was readiness to listen to his direction, while at the same time questioning his authority.

What was Secretary Haig trying to accomplish? Was he seeking to seize power? I don't think so. I personally believe that Secretary Haig was trying to handle the crisis and help the nation weather the storm. He should have, however, contacted Vice President Bush. Bush then could have decided to address the nation. Perhaps the action revealed something about the character of Secretary Haig. He didn't really know how to lead effectively. He tried to *control* the environment by controlling people's responses. He was trying to say, "It is OK." He was trying to calm people down. But, it wasn't all right. The leader of our nation had been shot. We were in a crisis. Misguided efforts at control were not the solution. They never are. I am not purporting to be a national leader or to know how to direct a country. But I believe that a better approach would have been for the one who had had jurisdiction simply to tell the truth.

Perhaps Bush could have said something like this, "President Reagan has been shot. He needs our prayers and support. The Cabinet is gathering to discuss the strategy we as a nation should pursue at this time. We need your prayers. There is no reason to fear. We live in a country where our constitutional form of government has provided for, and God forbid that it becomes necessary, an easy succession of power. We have every reason to believe that President Reagan will recover. In the meantime, the business of government will go on."

But Secretary of State Haig tried to control the situation and he failed. So it is with many of us. We seek to control people or situations and we fail.

WE CAN'T CONTROL OUR EMOTIONS, OUR ENVIRONMENT, OR OTHERS

In my own life, I have tried to control things. All such attempts have been abysmal failures. Perhaps they date back to the summer after fourth grade when I experienced the significant trauma of seeing the house we were living in literally blow up and burn to the ground.

I remember coming home that day and running up the long flight of stairs. My brother and I left our shoes on the landing. We were attracted by the aroma of chicken cacciatore coming from the kitchen. We sat at the table and began to enjoy our meal. My father was particularly jovial that evening, and we were all enjoying the shared family laughter.

All of sudden that scene of joy was interrupted by a scream from downstairs. "There's a fire! There's a fire!" My father sternly looked at us all and told us to grab nothing and head for the front door. I watched everyone flee as he turned and ran downstairs to assist the woman who lived below us. He didn't know I was watching. I saw him knock on her door. She stood there in tears with her children beside her. My father opened the basement door and fire singed his hair and his eyebrows. He picked up her children and took her out. He then saw me and yelled, "Get out that front door." I did. We all made it out just in the nick of time.

The firemen at that point had arrived. Though it was a rainy and gloomy evening, that didn't stop the ravages of this uncontrollable fury of smoke and flame. I sat in a car to try to keep dry and began to weep uncontrollably. I looked at our home and saw flames literally shooting up the walls. There were firemen on the roof. One of them fell in. Then what appeared to be a mushroom of flames engulfed the entire house. Fortunately all of the firemen escaped without serious harm, but the house was reduced to ashes.

Because we in the family never talked about the fire, or the fear associated with it, in my own immature way I tried to control my fear. How did I do this? I pushed it down. I suppressed it. However, emotions have a funny way of resurfacing when you try to suppress them. Young as I was, I gave the illusion of being in control. I seemed very mature for my age. But inside I was a frightened child. As the years passed, the fear itself began to control me. At times of crisis, pain, and struggle in my family life, I controlled my emotional reactions.

In my teenage years I went through intense rebellion. The primary emotion I manifested at that time was anger. However, I wasn't really feeling anger. It was a smoke screen for my true feelings. I was feeling deep-seated and unresolved hurt, abandonment, and resentment. But I controlled all of that with the emotion of anger.

I fit right in with the growing, seething corporate anger of the late sixties. Rather than looking inside myself, I directed my anger outward at whatever symbol of the establishment I could find. I rebelled against the leadership of my father. I rebelled against the leadership being provided by then President Richard Nixon. I perceived it as no leadership. I was angry at what I was being told about the military-industrial complex. I was angry at the way the establishment seemed to be treating antiwar demonstrators and those who were trying to create a counterculture. That is not to say there weren't some legitimate things to disagree with in both spheres of leadership—my family's and my nation's.

But what was wrong was something deep inside of me—a wound that needed healing. My coping mechanism of control enabled me to avoid dealing with the deep-seated feelings inside me.

Similarly, I have had a weight problem most of my life. I have been the inveterate "yo-yo" dieter. However, even at the peak of dieting, in slim-and-trim physical condition, I never really dealt with the source of my eating problem.[3] My diets—and they were varied and exotic—were superficial efforts at controlling the deep emptiness within. While I was dieting, I actually thought I was controlling my eating problem, but I really wasn't. The kind of control we are talking about is an illusion. Operating oftentimes with its cousins, denial and avoidance, it does not produce positive results.

I also controlled my pain. How? One example was my reaction to the illness and impending death of my dear friend, Fr. Philip. I controlled my emotions by pretending it wasn't happening. I had picked up this controlling approach almost by osmosis in my family. However, I have come to discover that many other people seek to control emotions, circumstances, and people in similar ways.

Control is indeed a learned reaction. It is a typical response when circumstances become unmanageable. When the inevitable painful realities of life overwhelm us, consciously or unconsciously, we decide to "white knuckle" it. We hope that by exercising our own willpower we will be safe. Or we hope that if we can control the behavior of others, our own lives will go better. But the very idea that we have such power over ourselves or others is an illusion.

Many of us have even grown to believe that we should control our own feelings by denying that they exist. But they do exist and can be our greatest allies. Though they can run amuck, when we are honest with ourselves, they can become guideposts and provide help along the way. But when we suppress them or deny they exist, rather than going away, they surface later in destructive ways.

The earliest example of this in my life is compulsive overeating. Its physical effect was obvious, but the more serious destruction was internal, in a place nobody could see. The shame, the poor self-image, and the lack of self-love have had a much deeper impact. You see, my deeper emotional problems wouldn't go away even when my excess weight went away. This faulty attempt at suppressing true feelings is another example of pretending that everything is OK, when we know in our gut that it really isn't.

In their wonderful book on dysfunctional families, John and Linda Friel talk about compulsive behavior:

> *A compulsion is something we do that we do not feel we are able to control or stop, but gives us the illusion of being in control.* The "out, out, damned spot" compulsive hand washing to try and remove some imagined sin from one's hands is a classic example of a compulsion. As would be getting up in the night seven or eight times to check to see if you locked all the doors and windows. Clinicians speak of compulsive overeating, compulsive gambling or compulsive cleaning and spending. Sound familiar? Am I a compulsive gambler or am I a gambling addict? It doesn't really matter what we call it, as long as we know that it is something out of control that is doing us and others harm.[4] **emphasis mine**

In his critically acclaimed national bestseller, *Bradshaw on: The Family*, John Bradshaw discusses the "covert rules" that often operate in families. Among them are control, perfectionism, blame, and denial of the five freedoms: "you shouldn't think, feel, desire, imagine, see or hear things the way you do."

He also recounts two common defense mechanisms which operate in families which are not dealing with their problems: the "no-talk rule" and reframing the hurt, pain, and distress of the past in an illusory, "myth-making" way. Bradshaw notes: "One must be in control of all interactions, feelings or personal behavior at all times. This is the cardinal rule of all dysfunctional, shame-based family systems. Control is the major defense strategy for shame. Once you control feelings, all spontaneity is lost. Control gives each member a sense of power, predictability and security. Control madness is a form of severe disability of the will since it tries to will away what cannot be willed away, [namely] the fundamental insecurity and unpredictability of life."[5]

Control can operate in a number of different ways in our lives. We may try to control people in an effort to control the environment around us and the response of others to us. Or we can try to suppress or deny our own emotions. But whichever way the illusion of control operates, its results can be devastating.

Jesus himself understood and experienced strong emotions. People who came to him were often in the midst of intense emotional pain and struggle. They would cry out and beg for his help. He never told them to suppress their emotions. He knew that strong emotions are not bad. People knew that Jesus was the kind of man they could express their feelings around. They felt safe in his presence and shared their pain with him. He experienced the deep emotion of loss and grief when he wept at the death of his friend Lazarus (Jn 11:33-35). There is a big difference between being mastered by disordered and confused feelings and allowing our emotions to have a proper role in our lives. By suppressing and not expressing them, our emotional health suffers. Such suppression of emotion can even lead to ulcers and compulsive behaviors over time.

Similarly, attempting to control others or one's environment can be destructive. Besides, it never works. Though environments that look controlled seem in good order, underneath the surface one can quickly see dissension and hypocrisy. In environments like this you find people complaining, backbiting, or acting out by living secret lives. This is the case whether that environment is at work, in the home, or, in some cases, at church.

Perhaps you have lived, worked, or worshiped in an environment where this kind of control has operated. People comply externally, but then behind closed doors complain bitterly. From a distance it may look efficient, but in reality it is often more dangerous to productivity then a seemingly disordered environment where honesty in relationships prevails.

Many psychologists, sociologists, and religious leaders have learned the truth of this modern-day phenomenon through counseling others in pain. When fear, anger, resentment, and other emotions are not properly dealt with, they can manifest themselves in destructive behaviors such as overeating and alcoholism.

All of this eventually catches up with us. For all too often it is the emotions we have suppressed which are trying to tell us the truth about our lives. We are simply not listening. Everything is not all right, and we need to face reality honestly. We need to admit our need. We need to confess our responsibility for hurting others or hurting ourselves. We need to repent of sin when we have objectively offended God and his people. Instead, we hide our heads in the clouds of control and enjoy a view that exists only in our minds.

This illusion of control can develop as a result of our having been reared in homes where denial reigns supreme. For example, it can develop in a home where substances—alcohol, drugs, food, even religion—are abused, but no one is honest enough to admit it and seek help. Or it can happen in a home where abuse reigns, whether physical, sexual, spiritual, or emotional.

However, control can also be learned later. For example, many are discovering that church groups, modeled as they are on the family system, can become abusive and dysfunctional,[6] contributing to the development of emotional illness, compulsive behaviors, and self-destructive patterns of control and denial even in people who were reared in otherwise healthy families.

In groups of this sort, the slide to denial and control is usually slow. They start out well-intentioned in their efforts to live fully the scriptural command to love one another in the context of a vibrant body of believers. However, for a lot of different reasons, leaders and rank-and-file members can begin to operate like an extended dysfunctional family.

After all, the church is populated by human beings who are many times frail, weak, and wounded. Fortunately, the divine power of the Lord, who is the head of the church, is also manifested in the midst of this frail, weak, and wounded human community. The great and grand mystery of the incarnation is that God became flesh and continues to manifest himself through the human community he calls to follow him.

These problems may occur not simply because the members of a group are weak and wounded, but because of failure of leaders and members to face problems honestly. Oftentimes that failure is couched in denial of problems or in control of the environment to minimize the appearance of any problems. A "no-talk rule" can develop within the group and then denial and control are free to grow. What is most frightening in such religious systems is that piety can be misused to hide problems. For instance, protecting leaders' reputations in the name of confidentiality can become a smoke screen for a failure to address real differences between leaders and members. Such a no-talk rule can lead to a significant lapse in accountability on the part of leaders to the very members they are committed to serve. The fact is, both families and church groups make mistakes that are often hidden and then compounded by denial and control.

This can happen even in a Catholic parish or in any church or para-church environment. After all, the church is indeed an extended family. When our own experience of family has not been adequate, we tend, consciously or unconsciously, to behave similarly in our efforts to build an extended family.[7]

Consider this example, which draws upon some of the common elements in abusive and dysfunctional churches. Fr. Ed arrived at his new suburban parish and quickly won over the congregation with his "Let's-get-things-done" style. His youth and vibrant personality particularly endeared him to the young people of the parish.

But soon parishioners began to see another side to Fr. Ed. While he celebrated Mass with great enthusiasm and was even known throughout the wider religious community for his inspirational sermons, he could be curt and controlling when he didn't get his way at parish council and staff meetings. He would even resort to sabotaging the leadership of those who didn't agree with him. Soon staff members, parish council members, and commission chairpersons began to resign and then even leave the parish. But Fr. Ed pointedly denied there was any leadership crisis, stating that he was simply getting rid of dead wood.

Meanwhile, Dick, the chairman of the parish council, had received some disturbing news from early, weekday-morning Massgoers. Fr. Ed was arriving at church early in the morning drunk. A couple of times he had even staggered and fallen on the sanctuary steps during Mass. When Dick discreetly confronted Fr. Ed with the parishioners' concerns, he flatly denied he had a drinking problem.

But as Dick probed deeper he learned the priest's father had been an alcoholic and had died of cirrhosis of the liver. He also learned in a phone conversation with Ed's mother that the father had been a strict authoritarian who had verbally abused his wife and children.

Armed with this information, Dick had a long talk with Fr. Ed. But again Fr. Ed denied almost everything, hotly contesting any comparison between himself and his father. Fr. Ed also began to avoid Dick and do everything he could to neutralize and sabotage his leadership on parish council. Even so, Dick and the entire parish council were sworn to secrecy about Fr. Ed's problems in an effort to protect his reputation. But this no-talk rule simply made parishioners assume the worst about Fr. Ed, based on innuendo and rumor.

Finally, in utter desperation, Dick made an appointment with the bishop. Of course, Fr. Ed was notified and attended the meeting as well. There he denied nearly everything and was largely exonerated.

To avoid any further problems, however, the bishop quietly transferred Fr. Ed to a parish in a small town. The thought was that Fr. Ed had been working too hard and a smaller, low-key parish would be a better match for his leadership style.

WHY WE ARE NOT IN CONTROL AND WHO REALLY IS

Whatever the root of unhealthy control, or wherever it is growing, the fruit is always bad. In fact, denial and control are two sides of the same worthless coin. They are coping mechanisms which pretend to buy freedom and manageability but instead turn out to be wooden nickels that have no real purchasing power.

For instance, one has to wonder whether the bishop wasn't enabling Fr. Ed to continue his addiction and perpetuate the same abusive style of leadership in another parish. Fr. Ed had denied most of Dick's charges and persuaded the bishop to believe his side of the story. Thus, Fr. Ed's pattern of denial and control had no real power to free him from his problems. Instead, it actually fueled the addiction and abusive leadership style which he had inherited from his father. The pattern would simply be repeated and Fr. Ed's problems would probably worsen in yet another parish.

In her outstanding book *Codependents' Guide to the Twelve Steps*, Melody Beattie adeptly describes the dilemma of control in her discussion of the "First Step" of a recommended Twelve-Step process for overcoming codependency. It is the antidote to illusory control.

> I love this Step. But I hate that I can't control. I hate being vulnerable and helpless. I don't like feeling uncomfortable or being in emotional pain. I get sick of having to detach and surrender. I am powerless over much in life, and when I try to have power where I have none, I get crazy. I can't control

others, no matter how much I want to, no matter how much better I think I know what's right for them.

... When I try to control other people, I make them and myself crazy. When I try to control addictions, the addictions control me. When I try to control what others think of me, I turn into a puppet on strings. Controlling makes me and others crazy. It puts me under the control of whatever I'm trying to influence. I lose myself. I lose touch with myself.

Controlling sets up a peculiar energy. People can feel it—even if we're just thinking about it and not acting on it. People react to it—sometimes by deliberately doing what we are trying to make them stop doing, or not doing what we are trying to make them do. It's an energy controlled by fear.[8]

The simple fact is, we are *not* in control, God is. Just as Secretary of State Haig was not in control of the White House, no matter how many people he told or how many millions viewed his claim on national television. The sooner we acknowledge our lack of control, our powerlessness, the sooner we can begin to experience the power of God. That is what surrender is all about. It's the beginning of freedom. We let go of control and let God rule.

The struggle we face is not new. It is the age-old struggle of the whole human race. Who is really in control? God created Adam and Eve and gave them an environment that was perfectly suited. He gave them a rich and meaningful life. He gave them purpose and intimate friendship with himself. The one thing he did not give them was control over the universe.

Yet when tempted by the fruit of the forbidden tree, they ate of it. They sought to take control from the one who has the only true right to it, the Living God. And then they sought to cover up their act. They pointed the finger of blame first at one another and then at the serpent. Their control and denial worked hand in glove. They ate of the forbidden fruit so that they and not God would control their destiny. The immediate result was denial when they were confronted by God and the loss of their destiny in the garden. Also they felt ashamed, covering their nakedness (Gn 3). Their misguided effort at control, the bad fruit of denial, and the loss of intimacy and honesty with God and each other have plagued the human race ever since.

One of the greatest deceptions we Christians can fall prey to is thinking that once we accept Jesus Christ as our Lord and return to the church, that's enough. The fact is we keep pushing him off his throne. Each time we do it, it becomes harder to recognize. We've become so smooth at rationalization. We've even developed spiritual language to make it look different. The problem is when we take back the throne, he can no longer rule. It is perhaps the most subtle and insidious deception of the Christian life.

Though this pattern of control goes way back in my own life, I didn't always recognize it. It was as though scales had to fall from my eyes before I could begin to see how deeply it had affected me. The scales fell off slowly. As shared in the last chapter, I experienced a profound conversion as a teenager which began the process of stripping them away.

Yet even though this conversion experience laid bare my heart both to the Lord and to myself, later experiences have had a funny way of quickly putting callouses back over my sensitive skin. With age, I began to see that of the scales I thought had fallen off completely, some were still present. The pattern of denial and control, which had begun very early, was still present. Conversion and surrender had to continue. Conversion is still continuing. Thank God it has and is. But it seems to me that there are special times when both because of his grace and our response, the Lord touches us deeply and transforms us in a significant way. These seasons or experiences of surrender and admission to God are what I call "evangelical moments."[9]

THE TWELVE STEPS AS A PATH TO CONVERSION

The Twelve Steps have helped me understand this conversion process as an antidote to denial and the illusion of control. Yet I have been saddened recently by the position taken by many Christian leaders who denigrate the use of the Twelve-Step process by recovery groups. While I can certainly appreciate their fear that the process itself could degenerate into one of blaming others and failing to take responsibility, I contend that if skeptics would simply explore the Twelve Steps themselves they would see that the steps are not the problem, but the fact that some people get stuck on a step of the ladder. In fact, these steps, which have been used countless times to help release people from various addictions, can be a path to authentic conversion.[10] Such an understanding and approach would help prevent people from getting stuck, because they would recognize the Twelve Steps as part of a process and not as an end in themselves.

Let me walk through the steps and show you exactly what I mean. In the first, we are asked to admit that we are powerless (whether it be over substances, people, or ourselves) and that our lives have become unmanageable.

In the second, we are called to believe that only a power greater than ourselves can restore us to sanity.

In the third, we are challenged to make a decision to turn our will and our lives over to the care of that Higher Power, whom we know is God.

In the fourth, we are asked to make a searching and fearless moral inventory of ourselves, much akin to the inventory that every Catholic should undertake before he or she makes a general confession.

In the fifth, we are asked to admit to God, to ourselves, and to another human being the exact nature of our wrongs. Again, this step is certainly akin to the model offered to us in the Sacrament of Reconciliation where the priest, as a representative of Christ and the community of the faithful, becomes an agent of healing, absolution, and restoration.

In the sixth, we are encouraged to be entirely ready to have God remove all of these defects of character. This is certainly akin to the Christian call to maturity and holiness.

In the seventh, we ask him humbly to remove our shortcomings. Again, this relates to the Christian call to maturity and personal responsibility.

In the eighth, we are asked to make a list of all the people we have harmed and become willing to make amends to them. Restitution is an important aspect of repentance and should follow a good confession of sins when those sins have harmed others in a way that calls for amends.

In the ninth, we make the amends, except when to do so would injure the person or others—simply good pastoral prudence.

In the tenth, we are called continually to take personal inventory and ownership of our lives. Also when we are wronged or have wronged someone to promptly resolve it—a path to ongoing conversion.

In the eleventh, we are encouraged to seek the Lord through prayer, asking for his will in our lives and for his power to guide us. This relates to the Christian call to daily prayer and seeking the Lord.

Finally, in the twelfth, we are told to share the spiritual awakening we have experienced with others. Certainly, this step is a powerful expression of evangelism.

While the Twelve-Step process may be misused by some, when properly followed, the steps do, in fact, lead to personal responsibility, authentic conversion, and maturity.

We have seen an interesting phenomenon in many Christian circles in recent years. Seemingly large numbers of believers are not finding the real-life support they need in their churches. I'm thinking here of family members who suffer from alcoholism and drug abuse and children who are being raised in single-parent families—to mention but a few. Such people are usually finding the support they need in Twelve-Step groups. Why?

At the risk of sounding overly simplistic, I would suggest that they have not experienced true mercy, understanding, and healing for their "nitty-gritty" problems at church. Yet the church is supposed to be the healing community—a community of sinners who are saved by the grace of God. It should be a spiritual hospital of sorts where people can meet God's mercy through the ministry of the body of Christ. But all too often we have lost sight of that aspect of the church's mission. Seeking to be a community of the perfect, we find little room for the wounded and the real problems people face at work, at home, and in school. Not only that, beyond healing, people should be experiencing authentic renewal and conversion at church. Yet it happens rarely. How unlike our Master that truly is! Time and again, in the Gospels, Jesus meets people at their point of need and leads them to conversion.

In encounters with people like the woman at the well, Zacchaeus the tax collector, and the woman caught in the act of adultery, Jesus is compassionate and heals a sinner at his or her deepest point of need. That healing becomes a true evangelical moment, leading a repentant sinner down the path of authentic conversion and renewal. How unlike many of our experiences of church!

Most Twelve-Step programs encourage the participant to find a "community of affiliation" within which to find and give support. What better community of affiliation should there be than the one inaugurated by the Good Shepherd? Yet too many Christians are finding judgmentalism, legalism, and authoritarianism instead of openness, mercy, and understanding within their parishes, congregations, and para-church groups.

The environment of a group is key. But often even that environment can be affected detrimentally by the illusion of control, as we saw in Fr. Ed's situation when the parish council instituted the no-talk rule to protect his reputation. Not only didn't it work, it made people assume the worst about Fr. Ed.

Sometimes the individual trying to exert control cannot change the people he or she leads, so that person seeks instead to change the atmosphere. In a sense, it should come as no surprise that many who lead groups exercise control in a destructive way. After all, we are all products of our past. Many of us have been raised in families where the grand illusion of control reigned supreme. Take Fr. Ed. He was raised by a strict, author-itarian father who verbally abused his family and was an alco-holic. He did not learn how to lead and to serve. So it is with many of us. The models that were supposed to demonstrate leadership and service at home were all too often deficient.

Let me share with you some of the things that happened in my own home. Again, I want to make clear that I love my par-ents and am grateful for much of what occurred in my child-hood. I do not blame them for anything. But in my efforts at being free from the illusion of control and finding peace through surrender, I had to deal with reality and not illusion.

HOW CONTROL AND MANIPULATION WORKED IN MY FAMILY

When I was a young boy, my grandfather lived with my fam-ily. His name was Maurice and I both loved and feared him. We lived in the top two floors of an older home in Dorchester, Massachusetts. In order to enter our apartment, you had to enter at the street level and then walk up a winding flight of stairs. I will never forget those stairs. Night after night, in the wee morning hours, my grandfather would pound on the front door at the bottom of the stairs. He was usually in a drunken stupor. Whenever we kids would wake up to see what was hap-pening, my mother would send us back to our rooms and tell us it was nothing. We knew better. Nothing doesn't occur at one in the morning.

Everything wasn't all right. My grandfather was captive to a disease more powerful than himself, and he was suffering deeply. Everyone around him was suffering as well. Though my mother was well-intended in her efforts to protect us, she was accomplishing the exact opposite by attempting to control the environment. That is a mistake we all make when we seek to control in this way. Her response was not unlike Secretary Haig's. She probably thought it was the best thing to do. After all, she had been raised in a home where the negative effects of this disease hadn't ever been resolved, so she passed on the same dysfunctional response of denial and control. What else could she have done?

She could have told us the truth. Something like, "Your grandfather has an illness. He is an alcoholic. Because we love him, we need to help him face his illness. We also need to be honest about the pain it causes each one of us. I know it's frightening, but we are in this together and God is with us." I love my mother. I admire the fact that she at least tried to handle the situation. However, none of us dealt with the situation very well. It dealt with us. And the cycle of denial and control that it unleashed continues in our own family life to this day.

After I left home, I discovered that this pattern of denial and control was deeply ingrained in me. When I was confronted with my own inadequacies, failures, and weakness, I would find myself clinging to the pattern like an old familiar shoe, rather than risking the discomfort necessary to face and confront problems.

One of the first living situations I found myself in after leaving home was in Newberry Port in Massachusetts. I had been invited to spend the summer with two friends. One of their fathers, a college professor, was in Europe for the summer. This friend, whom I'll call Charlie, was the product of a single-parent home. I had met him and another friend I'll call Henry in school. They both fancied themselves as hippies as did I at the time. The summer experience sounded like a lot of fun. There were three bedrooms in the house, so we chose which one would be ours by lot.

Fortunately, I got Charlie's father's room which was filled with books by great heroes of Christianity like C.S. Lewis, George MacDonald, and G.K. Chesterton. Reading those books that summer was a tremendous protection for me. You see, it turned out that Henry was a practicing warlock. I know that for many of you that may sound absurd. At the time I thought it was just a joke, but as the summer went on, his mannerisms and manipulative behavior became increasingly sick.

I didn't know how to cope, so I sought to control the environment and deny that it was happening. I spent less and less time in the house. Then I left without notice. This kind of flight in the face of difficulty became a pattern in my early adulthood.

In the case of my grandfather, because I was the youngest of three children at the time, I didn't know how to cope with the presence of active alcoholism in my home. The tension, the shouting, and the deception were all hard enough. But only years later would I come to see that worse than all of them was the miserable and failed attempt at denial and control.

My grandfather drank wine, bottle after bottle. He would hide it in different places around the house, and most of us knew at least three of those stashes. While his addiction created great tension, so did his unpredictable moods. I never knew what I would find in the morning—a kind, loving, gray-haired man drawing me pictures of roosters and cooking me eggs over easy, or a drunken and angry old man growling at me. I loved him nonetheless.

In my young impressionable mind I couldn't understand why he treated me like he did. But I did know that I loved him. I still do. I thought it was my fault, that somehow I wasn't a "good boy," and I didn't measure up. My mother has always laughed about my early childhood habit of introducing myself as "Keith Fournier, good boy." But it was rooted in this unwarranted sense of blame and shame. Though my introduction was humorous to my mother and many others, it was tragically symptomatic of the root of a problem which would affect me for many years—perfectionism.

This effort to be perfect continued in later struggles to live a good, Christian life. I was tailor-made for legalism, and I bought it hook, line, and sinker. I wanted to show everyone, including God, that I was really good and worthy of love. I now look back and see how sad that was. Little did I know that hunger for affirmation and approval would affect me well into my thirties.

My mother never fully acknowledged Grandpa's problem,

and neither did the family. This is not unusual for a daughter of an active alcoholic. She fit the classic pattern of caretaking and codependency.[11]

Pushing down her own emotions and fears, she denied and controlled. We followed her example and did the same. But Grandpa just kept drinking, and the problems unleashed in the family didn't go away. They got steadily worse. He drank himself to death from cirrhosis of the liver. To this day I don't even remember the funeral. So intense was the pattern of denial and control in our home that I still haven't recovered many memories from my early years. The secret of Grandpa, as with the explosion and fire that gutted our home, was kept and we never talked about it.

In reaction to these dysfunctional patterns in my family of origin, I developed, among other patterns, a tendency to pretend that real problems did not exist or to spiritualize them after my conversion. I'm not saying that there isn't a spiritual dimension to most of the difficulties in our lives. However, spiritualizing in this sense was one more way of denying and controlling for me. Why? Because I would very often fail to confront the problem at its source. For example, a difficulty in a relationship between a family member and me, or the reality of struggle as my wife and children sought to cope with an increasingly difficult home environment, was seen as only a spiritual attack of the evil one.

Additionally, within our home a no-talk rule began to develop. Though perhaps not as extreme as my family of origin, it was sometimes even more problematic. Why? Because again it was spiritualized. I would simply tell the children that some of their emotional experiences were wrong and that we didn't need to talk about these things. They simply needed to start acting differently. But there is nothing simple about that. In fact, it is important for human beings to express their feelings and views. That should be part of a healthy family environment.

I began to develop a rigidity in my leadership at home. Rules were replacing empathy and understanding. In short, like

Captain Von Trapp in "The Sound of Music," I appeared to be producing perfect kids. They would say the right things, do the right things, and obey. But their hearts were hurting. Thank God for their mother and thank God for the Holy Spirit helping us realize the truth. Laurine during this time began to see the problems before I did. She, like Maria in the "Sound of Music," helped to prevent even more harm coming to our children.

Denial and control can cause us to behave in compulsive ways. When we attempt to thus control life, we avoid facing the truth. Such attempts may result in self-destructive behavior patterns such as compulsive overeating. Or we may abuse drugs and alcohol. At some point, either through confrontation, or sometimes failure, we have to face the truth of our condition. The truth is that the way to deal with struggle, hurt, pain, failure, and difficulty is not through denial or control, but through honest acknowledgment, surrender, admission, and seeking forgiveness and recovery. We must begin by cultivating inner honesty.

One cold day in March years ago I awakened in a deep depression. The grayness of the sky reflected the grayness of my mood. It was another in a seemingly endless string of days that had grown into months during which I had become increasingly depressed. A number of pressures and hurts had lined up like well-aimed bowling balls, knocking over all my carefully placed pins. My professional career and self-esteem were at an all-time low.

THE COMPULSIVE BEHAVIORS
THAT RULE OUR LIVES

A big part of the problem was that I had been taking great pride in my own accomplishments. This goes hand in glove with a low self-image and perfectionism. I had been successful in almost everything I had tried. Of course, much of what I accomplished was God's blessing and calling. However, I also believe that it was in large part motivated by my own self-will.

Using our self-will as a source of power leads to pride, the greatest of sins. Pride had become my ally. In my steady climb toward success, I had assumed increasing responsibility in both ministry and career activities.

Another problem that is symptomatic of people like me is the inability to say no. I have learned to say no only in the last couple of years. On the professional front, I had inherited all the responsibilities of a fellow employee who seemed to have contracted chronic fatigue syndrome and had taken an extended leave of absence. His work had been left a virtual wasteland. Every project was slated for failure, and in fact, each one did.

Though I had taken over his responsibilities by default and for only a very short time, nonetheless, I took the blame. For the first time in my professional life, it looked as if I had failed. My perfect record had been shattered. My sense of accomplishment had been severely deflated.

Additionally, I had been involved in lay pastoral work, evangelism, and ministry almost all of my adult life. It was the most important thing next to my family. Mostly I got involved because I deeply loved, and still love, the Lord Jesus Christ. However, over the years that love for the Lord had faded as the primary motivation. I would only later see that much of my striving merely fueled my insatiable need for affirmation and success.

Over several months, I had been confronted by people for whom I had pastoral responsibility and with whom I had shared many years of ministry and service. I was convinced I had done a great job helping these dear people follow the Lord and resolve their problems. But they confronted me with a very different story. They told me that I was controlling, harsh, and, though probably well-intentioned, had contributed to their problems rather than helped alleviate them. The pain of those confrontations was like a deep, aching wound in my life.

In one instance, the wife of a man whom I was forming for

leadership in lay ministry, confronted me about my harshness and spiritual abuse of her husband. Her husband never said a thing, probably out of fear. Angrily, she accused me of not caring. While it hurt me deeply, much of what she said rang true. Of course, at the time, I thought I was helping her husband develop manly character and solid leadership skills—not to be bound by emotions, including her own. But, in reality, I was misguided in my efforts.

Not too long after this experience, another couple came to my office and they asked to speak with me. I could see by the somber looks on their faces that they had a grave matter to share with me. Something in my heart told me this was the Lord's doing. As I listened to their pain, I realized that I had contributed to it. Though I was not the only one, I knew that I had to own up to my responsibility for what had happened. This man had also been under my leadership for a short time. During that time, I had applied the same kind of misguided authoritarian leadership.

I sincerely apologized to these people, and they graciously forgave me. We shed tears together. One of the most wonderful fruits of the entire encounter was a friendship that endures to this day. How quick to forgive they were.

Over the next few months as I reviewed my life, I found that I had many people to visit whom I had harmed through my approach to leadership. The process was both painful and liberating. Dealing with denial and control honestly always is. In the past, however, my response to such people had been to minimize their comments and minimize my responsibility as well.

The residue of those encounters still pained me deeply on that cold day in March. I had been forced to reconsider everything I thought about my own leadership and how I had helped people over the years. I came to discover that much of my efforts to help were nothing less than caretaking.

The phrase "caretaking" is used in the recovery community to refer to an unhealthy way of taking care of others. As opposed to caregiving, caretaking is a controlling behavior whereby we make the other person's decisions for him or her. Rather than support the person's own self-care and empower him or her, we actually begin intervening and taking over the person's life.

My approach was similar to what I had seen in efforts to help throughout my upbringing, especially in my mother's caretaking of my grandfather. In addition, my failures in ministry forced me to reexamine many of my deeply held convictions regarding pastoral practice and spirituality. It was a frightening time.

Finally, I began to see the depth of my inadequacies as a father. In lay ministry, teaching on family was second only to evangelism. As the father of five children and husband of a wonderful wife, I took a certain pride in applying what I taught to life in my own home. Yet as my oldest child became a teenager, I began to see that my theory and practice didn't always go hand in hand.

For years I had served the equivalent of a full-time job in lay ministry plus two full-time career jobs, along with trying to be an effective husband and father. All of the pillars upon which I had built my false sense of security came tumbling down around me. I was exhausted and desolate. I began to drink wine almost nightly in a misguided effort to escape my pain.

Then that cold and dark March afternoon, a loud and insistent knock came to my front door. When I opened it, two men who had played important roles in my life solemnly asked to speak with me. We walked into the middle of the living room, suffused with gray light from the outdoors, where they confronted me.

"Keith, we believe you have a drinking problem," they said earnestly. My wife was present and I saw the deep concern on her own face.

"Could it be?" I asked myself. "Alcoholism has deeply affected my family," I told myself. "After all, I am drinking a lot these days." By the grace of God, I had now learned that denial was never the solution to my problems.

"Maybe you're right," I said. "Maybe I do have a drinking problem. I know I've been drinking a lot lately. What do you think I should do?" They then gave me a litany of advice, some of which proved helpful, most of which did not.

Later that evening one of these men took me to dinner. He then invited me to attend an Alcoholics Anonymous meeting. With great trepidation, but with a sincere and contrite desire to find out if I had succumbed to this disease, I accepted. I was immediately impressed with the honesty of the group. They told their life stories without any pretense. They owned up to their problems. They were humble in seeking help. Here was the inner honesty I craved.

It was time for introductions and about ten people preceded me. Over and over I heard, "My name is _____, and I am an alcoholic." When it came to me, however, I realized I could not say that because it wasn't true. "My name is Keith, and I appreciate being here tonight." I could see the look in the face of the friend who had accompanied me. A recovering alcoholic himself, he was disappointed. Apparently he was convinced I was an alcoholic. I was open to the possibility, but I also had to be honest with myself. Within the next week, I received much advice from well-intended people. But when all was said and done, I had to face myself. And I did so at a deeper level than ever before. What was wrong with me? What was I trying to escape?

MY RECOVERY

I finally began to see clearly the impact that my family of origin had had upon me and the pattern of denial and control that I had been using over the years.

As my recovery began, I read many recovery books under the advice of a counselor. I was intrigued by their discussion of what is often referred to as "the repetition cycle." This refers to the tendency of those from a dysfunctional family to repeat the very problems that existed in their family of origin.[12] I realized this was true of me.

My grandfather was an alcoholic. His compulsive drinking became a dangerous addiction. My mother was a compulsive overeater and had a pattern of caretaking in relationships. My father did not know how to deal with his anger and consequently attempted to control the home environment instead. Here I was, repeating some of those behaviors. I was over-indulging in food and drink. I was caretaking people around me—at home, at work, and in ministry. I was acting as a controlling father figure in leadership.

Many of those who have studied the dysfunctional family point out that children can assume roles. Roles such as "scapegoat," "victim," and "hero." I had included them all in my repertoire. No longer was I, in a healthy way, directing my own life. I was being directed by a life that had become unmanageable.

My depression did not diminish but deepened. Although I immediately stopped drinking, I could not shake my darkness and despair. I sought professional counseling. That was quite a decision for me. For years I had thought that counseling was unnecessary in most cases, that it could become a dangerous substitute for good spirituality. I had spoken against what I thought was the therapeutic mentality of the age. But I had to eat my own words.

With the help of a wonderful counselor, I began to explore what I can only explain in words from the popular television show *Star Trek*, as an area within me "... where no man has ever gone before." I discovered years of repressed memories. I began to remember many of my traumas from early childhood—the influence of my grandfather and the fire that gutted our family home. I began a journey inward and back to my beginnings.

I was surprised at what I found. After all, I had said many prayers for inner healing since my conversion as a teenager. I thought I had worked through everything and that the Lord had taken care of it all. Well, the Lord had taken care of what I had given to him, but still more was locked up inside.

As a part of my program of recovery, twice I saw the psychiatrist who was responsible for the counselor working with me. When my dark depression did not subside, he concluded I was suffering from clinical depression. He wrote out two prescriptions. One was for Prozak, a popular anti-depressant. He told me to carry them with me, and if I felt it was necessary, to take them. He spent much time explaining that none of this should be a cause of shame.

Thankfully, the prescriptions were not necessary. But I still to this day, as a memory of that time, carry those prescriptions. They are no longer valid, but they always remind me of my bottoming out. I never want to forget that.

Along with the counseling, I began to attend a Twelve-Step group to resolve codependency issues and those related to having been raised in a dysfunctional family. Though I realized that I was not addicted to any substance, I did tend to escape from difficulty. I escaped through overeating. And I had tried to escape through overindulging in wine. I saw as well that I was overly dependent upon people, especially leaders to make decisions for me. Indeed, I was looking to them for more and more direction.

I was overly dependent as well upon others for affirmation. That deep hole in my soul had re-emerged. Oh, how deep it went! Of course, the most obvious problem was my codependent relationship with food. I had ballooned to two hundred and fifty pounds. I needed to confront my compulsive overeating.

Such suffering and struggle usually accompany recovery and renewal. Though I learned I was not and am not an alcoholic, I do know the danger I face as an adult child[13] of alcoholism. I have to be very careful of compulsive overeating and very careful about any kind of substance which could become misused. I use the word "substance" quite loosely here. It can mean anything from chemicals and food, to philosophies, such as religion or misguided piety. In other words, even very good things can become the source of a codependency.

THE WAY OF THE CROSS

Years later I look back at that time of recovery and honest admission as a season of grace and conversion given by the Lord himself. I remember one particular discussion with my counselor. "Keith," he said, "you have spent much of your life climbing mountains of your own choosing. You have come down from them as well. Each time you have gotten very close to hitting bottom. But each time you have built a bridge over to the other mountain. Finally, you've crashed through that bridge. No matter how hard it seems now, you will thank God for it someday."

He was right. I had hit bottom in a way that I had never hit bottom before, and I did become grateful. Only then could I see my own desperate and continual need for God's mercy and grace. Only then could I finally see the wonderful height of the Cross of Calvary. It does indeed form a bridge between earth and heaven, and it leads all the way to the heart of a loving Father.

Unlike Secretary of State Haig, Fr. Ed, my mother, or so many other well-intentioned people, the Son of God did not say everything is all right. God sent his Son to confront the bad fruit of sin and rebellion. God saw us sin and rebel. The evidence demands a verdict: guilty as charged. But the sentence is lifted because Jesus ransomed us on the cross, and the condemned are allowed to share life everlasting with God.

The cross is the place where justice and mercy meet. He who knew no sin paid the penalty for our sin and opened the floodgates of mercy and forgiveness. The road to experiencing that mercy and forgiveness is one which we must continually travel. It is marked by the guideposts of admission and surrender, not denial and control. It is the narrow road of the cross. We simply are not God. Adam and Eve and everyone since the fall who has denied and tried to control are wrong about that. We cannot control our own lives, let alone those of others. But there is a "Higher Power."[14] The good news is that this Higher Power has revealed himself in Jesus Christ, his only Son.

God loved us so much (Jn 3:16) that he chose not only to be known simply as a Higher Power, but to be known, loved, and experienced as a person. He took on flesh and we have beheld his glory (Jn 1:14). He walked among us and experienced our pain, struggle, failure, and difficulty. And though he himself knew no sin (2 Cor 5:21), he took the penalty of our sin upon himself so that he could clothe us with the freedom and dignity of the son's and daughters of God. That is good news!

There is a way out of the illusion of control: surrender to him who is the Way, the Truth, and the Life (Jn 14:6)—the one who is really in control, anyway.

Denial and control, even once they are recognized, will sometimes rear their ugly heads in our lives. They are enemies that most of us never totally defeat. But in the words of St. Paul, "Indeed, we live as human beings, but we do not wage war according to human standards; for the weapons of our warfare are not merely human, but they have divine power to destroy strongholds..." (2 Cor 10:3-4).

The greatest ongoing weapon against control that I have found is to follow the way of the cross. In the Catholic tradition, a powerful Lenten devotion that focuses on this is called the "Stations of the Cross." As Christians reflect on the path to Calvary, they see how Jesus humbled himself and became powerless for our sake. Paul instructed the Christians in Philippi, "Let the same mind be in you that was in Christ Jesus, who, though he was in the form of God, did not regard equality with God as something to be exploited, but emptied himself, taking the form of a slave, being born in human likeness. And being found in human form, he humbled himself and became obedient to the point of death—even death on a cross" (Phil 2:5-8).

On his way of the cross, Jesus was not steely and controlled. He was a "man of sorrows and acquainted with grief" (Is 53, RSV). He reached out along the way to the women of Jerusalem (Lk 23:27). On the cross itself, he reached out in compassion and mercy to Dismas, the good thief (Lk 23:39-43). He manifested the depth of his love for his mother and the beloved disciple, John, at the peak of his pain. "Standing near the cross of Jesus were his mother, and his mother's sister, Mary the wife of Clopas, and Mary Magdalene. When Jesus saw his mother and the disciple whom he loved standing beside her, he said to his mother, 'Woman, here is your son.' Then he said to the disciple, 'Here is your mother.' And from that hour the disciple took her into his own home" (Jn 19:25-27).

Finally, in his last moments, about the ninth hour, he gave vent to his anguish and sense of powerlessness when he cried out, "*Eli, Eli, lama sabachthani,*' that is, 'My God, my God, why have you forsaken me?'" (Mt 27:46). In the last moments of his earthly life, Jesus showed us the way to live freely and fully, even when facing the deepest pain and anguish of soul. Jesus has showed us the way of honesty and humility. We can reflect on Jesus' humility and honesty in the devotion of the "Stations of the Cross." These same virtues are what we need to cultivate in overcoming denial and control.

These are the stations on which we meditate:

1. Jesus is condemned to death.
2. Jesus bears his cross.
3. Jesus falls the first time.
4. Jesus meets his mother.
5. Simon of Cyrene helps Jesus carry his cross.
6. Veronica wipes the face of Jesus.
7. Jesus falls the second time.
8. Jesus meets the women of Jerusalem.
9. Jesus falls the third time.
10. Jesus is stripped of his garments.
11. Jesus is nailed to the cross.
12. Jesus dies on the cross.
13. Jesus is taken down from the cross.
14. Jesus is placed in the tomb.

And we follow each meditation with this prayer, reaffirming our faith:

We adore you, O Christ,
and we praise you;
because by your holy cross,
you have redeemed the world.

So too, in the traditional morning offering, Catholics offer up the suffering and sorrow that is part of daily life in these words:

O Jesus, in union with your most Precious Blood poured out on the cross and offered in every Mass, I offer you today my prayers, works, joys, sorrows and sufferings for the praise of your Holy Name and all desires of your Sacred Heart; in reparation for sin, for the conversion of sinners, the union of all Christians and our final union with you in Heaven. Amen.

In our daily examination of conscience at the end of the day, we honestly acknowledge our faults and sins, taking responsibility for our actions:

Before examination of conscience
Lord Jesus Christ, judge of the living and the dead, before whom I must appear one day to give an exact account of my whole life, enlighten me, I beseech you, and give me a humble and contrite heart, that I may see wherein I have offended your infinite majesty and judge myself now with such a just severity that then you may judge me with mercy and clemency.

After examination of conscience
My God, I detest these and all other sins which I have committed against your divine majesty. I am sorry that I have offended you, because you are infinitely good and sin displeases you. I love you with my whole heart, and firmly purpose, by the help of your grace, never more to offend you. I resolve to avoid the occasions of sin; I will confess my sins and endeavour to make satisfaction for them. Have mercy on me, O God, have mercy, and pardon me, a

wretched sinner. In the name of your beloved Son, Jesus, I humbly beg you to wash me with his precious blood so that my sins may be entirely remitted.

But not only do I need to face daily my tendency toward denial and control, I need to strip off the mask of another ugly enemy of spiritual maturity—avoidance. A close relative to denial and control, avoidance is usually the bad fruit of both. It makes sense, doesn't it, to avoid what we deny and seek to control? The problem is it just makes things worse.

Avoidance—
It Just Makes
Things Worse

*Why do today what you can put off until
tomorrow?* —Joe

S UDDENLY, THERE WAS A LOUD POP. Then
the engine died in a burst of smoke.
Joe and I just looked at one another, first in shock and then in
grave disappointment. He managed to steer the car off the
road. We had to push it over onto the shoulder of the highway.
It was a 1965 Ford that we had purchased less than four hundred miles back. We were making our way across the country.
Like many other decisions we had made along the way, this one
had been stupid as well.

You see, the person who sold us the car didn't even have the
paper work. For all we knew, he didn't have the right to sell us
the car. But we were pleased by the purchase price of only fifty
dollars. It was better than hitchhiking. During the last five hundred miles, we had talked about our future in California. When
we finally arrived in this new land of opportunity, we would
make our dreams come true. We even talked about the car. We
discussed the possibility of making it into a convertible. We had
sketched out the design of our newly remodeled roadster. The
problem was, what would we do now?

Within a matter of minutes, Joe began to laugh uncontrollably. I joined suit. In the midst of what was a very difficult situation, the two of us were literally in stitches. We had to sit down by the side of the road and hold our stomachs we were laughing so hard. Finally, when the hysteria subsided, we had to face reality. But Joe never liked facing reality. "Joe, we need to call a tow truck," I said.

"No, we don't. The car's not worth it," Joe smirked.

"Well, what are we going to do?" I asked.

"Leave it by the side of the road. Maybe somebody else will use the parts," he responded.

Well, we did just that. We left our fifty-dollar car by the side of the road, stuck out our thumbs, and continued our journey. Some twenty years later, when I look back on the incident, I realize how irresponsible it was. We didn't even know who rightfully owned the car. We didn't know what was going to happen to it. But we had avoided what Joe always called "the hassle of life." Though I now disagree with his philosophy, Joe is still my friend. Joe and I spent most of our teenage years together in a little town named Sharon in Massachusetts. We were wayward pilgrims searching for something to believe in. Our search led us many places and eventually culminated in this cross-country journey that was both frightening and maturing. Joe loved to celebrate, party, dance, and basically enjoyed having a good time.

Filled with anecdotes, Joe could bring out a chuckle in anyone. "Why do today what you can put off until tomorrow?" was his theme song. A recipe for procrastination? Yes, but even more, a good summary of how avoidance can work in our lives. Like denial and control, avoidance doesn't work at all, but tends to make things worse.

We often fear the very things we need to face, so we avoid them. Some of us fall into the avoidance trap quite young. I did. Until the fifth grade, I lived in the inner city of Boston known as Dorchester, a congested urban area, where the kids learned to adjust and turned the streets into playgrounds. One of our favorite pastimes was stick ball. The kid who had the best mop stick got to be up first.

One day at the ripe old age of nine, I ventured outside my immediate neighborhood and traveled down toward Codman Square. Just off Norfolk Street a group of kids were playing stick ball. It was a narrow street that ran by the side of a brick tenement. Each side of the street was lined with old cars and the gutters were littered with candy wrappers, Coke cans, and smashed beer bottles. But it looked like fun. The kids invited me to join them.

When my turn came at bat, I swung with everything in me, trying to impress them all. To my amazement, I hit the ball! It seemed to soar beyond my sight, and I ran like crazy. Rounding second base with my eyes on third, I made the split-second decision to "go for it." I darted past a rusted jalopy with a piece of chrome trim hanging off it. The trim caught in the bend of my elbow. Overcome with fervor at showing my stuff, yet experiencing pain, I continued to run, ripping the chrome trim right off the car. I then pulled the piece of chrome out of my arm, which began to bleed profusely.

Most of the kids were scared that I was seriously injured, but even more afraid because the owner of that jalopy was a mean old man. They told me I had better run before I got into trouble. I raced to "Nat's" in my old neighborhood, a local store that was a favorite with the kids because Nat sold used penny comic books, penny candy, and big dill pickles for only a nickel. Nat was a kind old man I felt I could trust. He "doctored me up." I went home but hid the injury from my parents for a long time. This nine-year-old figured he faced a jail term if he ever got caught! I avoided that street for two years rather than face the consequences of what I had done.

Years later we moved to Sharon, a suburb on Boston's south shore. New to the town and a city kid to boot, I had a hard time fitting in. When I finally did find some friends, the first thing they told me about was the old lady who lived on Elm Street. "She's a witch," they said. "Don't ever let her catch you outside of her house." The problem I faced was that in order to reach a small shopping center named Sharon Heights where we all hung out, I had to go the long way on Main Street or take the short cut and pass this old woman's house.

I'll never forget the first time I took the shortcut with my newfound friends. We went through the underground train tunnel and came up right in front of her yellow, framed house. Much to my shock and dismay, my companions yelled out, "Come on out, old witch!" Then they broke away at a tear. Startled, I followed their lead, but because I wasn't aware of their strategy, I was the last one to leave, so I got caught. Out of the house ran this little old lady with fire in her eyes. "Hey, boy!" she yelled at me, "you come back here right this minute." I ran and ran and ran, terrified to death. For a chubby kid, I think I could have broken the mile record that afternoon.

When we all finally arrived at the shopping center, my friends laughed off the incident. I didn't. I felt terrible over what I had done. For months I avoided the shortcut to Sharon Heights. Why? Because I wanted to avoid the lady. I wanted to avoid facing the consequences of my actions.

A year later, I summoned up enough courage to walk by her house alone. Sure enough, she was outside raking her lawn. I walked right over to her and said, "Ma'am, I'm one of the boys who ran by your house last year. They yelled a bad name at you and ran. I'm sorry, I won't do it again."

She looked at me doubtfully. "Well, son," she said, "I'm from Missouri." I didn't understand what she meant. But I quickly perceived there was not going to be any more conversation. So I left, respectfully, bowing out of an awkward situation.

Only later when I asked my mother what the phrase, "I'm from Missouri," meant did I come to understand this woman was saying, "I'll believe it when I see it." I passed by her house many more times and soon developed a relationship with her.

One day she even invited me into her yard and showed me her prize rose collection. She explained to me how flowers respond to proper nutrients and regular watering. Soon I looked forward to my trips past her house. No longer was I a threat to her or she a threat to me. Our paths had crossed and we had become friends. Rather than avoiding the consequences of my action out of ignorance and fear, I had faced the piper and made a new friend.

AVOIDANCE: A FAMILY PATTERN

It's human to avoid the unpleasant and painful. Also we fear taking responsibility for our failures and wrongdoing, and our fear often leads to avoidance. Having grown up in a financially insecure family, I learned to fear bills. As an adult, this fear crippled me in managing a household budget. I would avoid paying off my debts. You can imagine the result. My financial problems simply got worse.

Concern about money set the atmosphere of my boyhood home. My father feared the Internal Revenue Service for years without any reason. We all feared bill collectors, but we had good reason for that.

One bitterly cold morning some men from a collection agency came and took my mother's car away. It was the first car that she had owned. She was working outside the home for the first time in many years, had lost weight, and was feeling good about herself. Though I didn't understand all that was happening to her, I could tell that it was positive. But that morning the joy of taking back her life seemed to drain completely out of her. We heard the car start and saw strange men driving it away. It was repossessed and we were never able to recover it. It was the beginning of a traumatic year.

Coming home from school in the middle of that winter, I saw my father atop a telephone pole with rubber gloves on. Our lights had been turned off so many times at the box that my father, who was trained as an electrician in the Navy, had learned how to turn them back on. So adept was he at this that the electric company disconnected our power at the pole. There he was, on a telephone pole, attempting to reconnect it himself. As you can imagine, I was in utter fear and amazement. The voltage could have killed him, but he was trying to take matters into his own hands so that we could have lights and heat.

That entire winter we used Coleman lamps to study by. We rented gas-powered generators whenever we could. I remember the illness caused by what I now believe was carbon monoxide in the house.

The summer after my fourth grade, we experienced the tragic explosion and fire that gutted the grand old house on Thetford Avenue in Dorchester, Massachusetts. My father was buying it on a land contract. Part of our monthly rent was credited toward the purchase. I remember my father renovating that house from top to bottom.

When he was painting the kitchen, he let the kids draw pictures on the wall before he primed it. One day we came home and he had drawn pictures of Narragansett beer bottles with the advertising slogan, "Have a Gansett." We all laughed at his artwork. He had refinished the old wooden floors in the house by stripping them on his knees—then sanding, restaining, and varnishing them. He rightly took great pride in his workmanship.

Unfortunately, he did not properly insure the house, so we lost everything in that tragic fire. Many of my father's hopes for the future literally went up in smoke as well. It also instilled in me a deep fear of fire. As I already mentioned, we never discussed the fire in our family. It simply got buried by our "no-talk rule."

This happens in a lot of families that never deal with significant events and concerns. The unresolved fear and pain don't go away, but eat away at family members. I had been an adult for many years before I came to see that my boyhood family was indeed as "sick as its secrets," a saying often heard in the recovery community.[1]

AVOIDANCE ONLY MAKES THINGS WORSE

Avoidance doesn't work because we can never truly avoid the consequences of our behavior. Why? Because the very things we try to avoid nonetheless affect us. We have to pay our bills and our taxes. We have to find shelter if our house is reduced to ashes. The difficulty we seek to avoid may be less dangerous than the pattern of avoidance we develop in response to it, since it can lead to lifelong compulsions and addictions.

Sometimes we try to avoid painful memories. For example, a very dear friend of my family has suffered for years with severe depression during the Christmas season. She is not alone. Statistics indicate that many suffer from depression around holidays. Generally, these people are pained by unresolved issues in their family life. Our friend tried to avoid the holiday altogether. She would literally go away during Christmas and pretend it wasn't happening.

Well, Christmas happens whether or not anyone pretends it doesn't. Holidays are a part of life. The effort to avoid them reminds me of how my three-year-old son, Joel, would close his eyes when he didn't like what his mom or I would say, particularly when he was being corrected. Joel thought that when he closed his eyes, we would go away. But we didn't, and neither do holidays.

Our friend finally got some help and began to realize that her efforts at avoiding Christmas were like closing her eyes. Oh, she had tried all kinds of justifications, including a burst of piety, saying she opposed the commercialization of Christmas. The real problem, though, was not Christmas, but her avoidance of deep-seated memories that were hurting her.

Recently, she celebrated Christmas with family and friends and was able to rejoice in the birth of Jesus Christ. How? By confronting her pain during Christmases past. She spent much time in deep and difficult conversations with her father about the death of her mother. As a result, years of wounds were exposed and ultimately healed through honest dialogue, tears, reconciliation, and forgiveness. Her recovery continues.

Birthdays and the aging process won't go away either. No matter how feverishly we try to pretend that we are not aging, our bodies tell us the truth. An entire industry has been built around deluding people into thinking that the aging process can be stopped or covered over. It all too often feeds a poor self-image in many of us. The adage is certainly true, there are at least two certainties in this life, "death and taxes." We simply will grow older, regardless of what Hollywood and Madison Avenue tell us.

Though we can seek to minimize our problems, we cannot avoid them by pretending they don't exist. I'm not saying that we should stop trying to minimize their impact. That would be foolish. If you were to receive a medical evaluation of a serious illness, you would seek treatment. We should seek healing from the Lord. He does heal! However, if illness continues, what often needs to change is our attitude of heart and response to being ill. So too with our personal struggles, including compulsive behavior patterns. Avoidance is never the solution. Rather honest acknowledgment, admission, surrender, and faith help us to overcome them. We even need to embrace the suffering, pain, and struggle when our problems won't seem to go away. The God of love can transform our suffering and struggle into wounds that heal. He understands our weaknesses.

EMBRACING OUR SUFFERING IN CHRIST

The author of the letter to the Hebrews reminds us: "For we do not have a high priest [Jesus] who is unable to sympathize with our weaknesses, but we have one who in every respect has been tested as we are, yet without sin. Let us therefore approach the throne of grace with boldness, so that we may receive mercy and find grace to help in time of need" (Heb 4:15-16). We who follow Jesus Christ have the greatest example for our own lives in the example of his humanity. Fully divine, yet fully human, he is intimately acquainted with our weaknesses. That is what we profess. Yet we all too often forget the humanity of Jesus. Jesus the man experienced the full panorama of human emotions. Still he did not sin. He teaches us how we can be both fully alive and fully free. He was tempted to avoid difficulty. Matthew the Evangelist writes of Christ's struggles to face the reality of the pain that awaited him:

Then Jesus went with them to a place called Gethsemane; and he said to his disciples, "Sit here while I go over there and pray." He took with him Peter and the two sons of Zebedee, and began to be grieved and agitated. Then he said to them, "I am deeply grieved, even to death; remain here, and stay awake with me." And going a little farther, he threw himself on the ground and prayed, "My Father, if it is possible, let this cup pass from me; yet not what I want but what you want." Then he came to the disciples and found them sleeping; and he said to Peter, "So, could you not stay awake with me one hour? Stay awake and pray that you may not come into the time of trial; the spirit indeed is willing, but the flesh is weak." Again he went away for the second time and prayed, "My Father, if this cannot pass unless I drink it, your will be done." Again he came and found them sleeping, for their eyes were heavy. So leaving them again, he went away and prayed for the third time, saying the same words. Then he came to the disciples and said to them, "Are you still sleeping and taking your rest? See, the hour is at hand, and the Son of Man is betrayed into the hands of sinners. Get up, let us be going! See, my betrayer is at hand."

Mt 26:36-46

In this moving account, we can see the anguish facing Jesus the man. Was it possible to avoid the cross? Was there another way? In the Gospel of St. Mark, this scene follows Jesus' prediction of Peter's denial (Mk 14:27-31). Not only had Jesus predicted Peter's denial, but he then demonstrated for Peter and for all of us that the way to overcome denial, control, and avoidance is to face reality as he did when confronting the cross. So intense was the pain and the struggle facing Jesus that the Evangelist Luke, recounting the same event tells us, "In his anguish he prayed more earnestly, and his sweat became like great drops of blood falling down on the ground" (Lk 22:44).

In his marvelous autobiography, *Treasure in Clay*, Bishop Fulton Sheen discusses avoidance in his own life. He refers to fear of the cross as "staurophobia." Bishop Sheen candidly acknowledges his own avoidance of suffering, and then shares about the open-heart surgery which opened his eyes.

God does not like unfinished symphonies or unfurled flags. In His mercy He will finish the temple we have left unfinished and clean and polish that which has remained unadorned. What we may regard as an evil may be actually a hidden good like the surgeon's use of a scalpel. He does not ask us if we will accept the finishing of the work His Father sent Him to do. He drafts us into His service as Simon the Cyrene that we might not be unripe and unplucked wheat in His Eucharistic sanctuary. He has many ways of tightening the violin strings that the priesthood may give forth a better harmony.

Since I would not take up the Cross, the Lord would lay it on my back as He laid it on Simon of Cyrene, who later came to love it. The cross took two forms: trial inside the Church and outside the Church. Eventually I came to see that the Lord was teaching me not only to be a priest, but also to be a victim. This explains why two of the books I authored are on this very subject.

I can remember when after four months in the hospital, I began to recover; I was reading Mass on an altar constructed over the bed before a few priests and friends. I spontaneously gave a sermon, which I remember so well. I said that I was glad that I had open-heart surgery because when the Lord comes to take us all, He will look to see if we have any marks of the Cross upon ourselves. He will look at our hands to see if they are crucified from sacrificial giving; He will look at our feet to see if they have been thorn-bruised and nail-pierced searching for lost sheep; He will look at our heart to see if that has been opened to receive His Divine Heart. Oh, what joy is mine just to have endured the minuscule imitation of His suffering on the cross by having a wounded side. Maybe He will recognize me from that scar and receive me into His kingdom.[2]

The cross is the place where human weakness and divine strength meet. It is indeed what Catherine of Siena called "the bridge between earth and heaven." When we confront our weakness and avoidance of pain with the attitude of faith and learn to embrace it, it can indeed sanctify us. This mystery is at the heart of the paradox of the gospel and the ancient Christian understanding of redemptive suffering.

In the early 1970s, I spent a year and a half as a religious postulant at a Benedictine monastery in Pecos, New Mexico. Young and on fire for the Lord, I wanted to go all out for him. After having rediscovered the beauty of my childhood faith in a teenage conversion, I sought to be rooted in the church and serve the Lord as a Catholic priest and a Benedictine monk.[3] The abbot of the monastery, David Gaerets, O.S.B., is a holy and wise man. Along with teaching me about the Eastern Fathers and Benedictine spirituality, he tried to teach me about the inevitability of suffering and struggle in every person's life.

But some things cannot be learned through words. They require experience and aging—not unlike a good wine. Jesus, in fact, compared the cup of suffering to wine, didn't he? When approached by the mother of Zebedee's sons, who wanted a position of honor for her offspring, Jesus responded: "'You do not know what you are asking. Are you able to drink the cup I am about to drink?' They said to him, 'We are able.' He said to them, 'You will indeed drink my cup, but to sit at my right hand or at my left, this is not mine to grant, but it is for those for whom been prepared by my Father'" (Mt 20:22-23).

What was that cup? The cup of suffering. Abbot David understood suffering. He authored a little pamphlet in the early 1970s on the "Baptism of Suffering," which restated the ancient Christian teaching on the redemptive role of suffering in the sanctification of believers. It was published, however, when the Catholic charismatic renewal was at its peak. People were experiencing in a new and fresh way the power of the Holy Spirit in their lives. Caught up in the euphoria, few wanted to hear about suffering. Things haven't changed much in two thousand years, have they?

Among the many wise things the Abbot would tell me, I will always remember: "The only difference between a Christian and an unbeliever when confronted with pain or death is how they respond to the inevitable. You can either embrace death or die like a stuck pig." At the time, his words seemed odd and

harsh to me. But their wisdom grows on me. After all, a numb-
ing fear of death is the ultimate in avoidance. If we can face
our death, we can face anything. Think of the stories of the
martyrs down through the ages—the dignity with which they
faced their earthly end, the openness and joy with which they
embraced pain. Obviously, they were given tremendous grace,
but they also understood the truth of the cross. They stopped
trying to avoid the unavoidable.

LEAVING OUR AVOIDANCE
AT THE FOOT OF THE CROSS

One of the ancient traditions about Peter involves his martyrdom and suggests that his pattern of denial and avoidance
didn't end with the ascension of the Master and the sending of
the Spirit, but right up to the day of his death. At the height of
the Roman persecution under Nero, many of the faithful fled
the city—Peter, among them. It is said that as he was leaving
the city gates, hoping to avoid martyrdom, he met the Master
walking past him into the city. Of course, he turned around
and followed the Master to the cross. Tradition adds that he
did not deem himself worthy to be crucified in the same manner as the Lord, so he was crucified upside down.

How can we also follow the Master to the cross, instead of
avoiding our trials? Among the many wonderful post-resurrection accounts recorded for us in the Gospels, the one that
stands out for me in this regard describes the experience of
two disciples traveling to a village called Emmaus, about seven
miles from Jerusalem (Lk 24:13-35). The Scripture tells us that
"while they were talking and discussing [the passion and death
of Jesus], Jesus himself came near and went with them but
their eyes were kept from recognizing him" (Lk 24:15-16).

During their interchange with this apparent stranger on the
road, their faces stayed downcast (Lk 24:17). They carried on a
sorrowful and pained conversation with this fellow traveler,
who listened to them opine about the events of the passion
and crucifixion of Jesus of Nazareth. He said to them, "'Oh,

how foolish you are, and how slow of heart to believe all that the prophets have declared! Was it not necessary that the Messiah should suffer these things and then enter into his glory?' Then beginning with Moses and all the prophets, he interpreted to them the things about himself in all the scriptures" (Lk 24:25-27). Even then, they did not recognize him.

When they reached Emmaus, the disciples invited the traveler to stay with them for the evening. It was only at table when he broke the bread that Scripture tells us, "Then their eyes were opened and they recognized him..." (v. 31). When they returned to Jerusalem they told the apostles what had happened: "Then they told what had happened on the road, and how he [Jesus] had been made known to them in the breaking of the bread" (Lk 24:35).

The breaking of the bread is symbolic of the Eucharistic Sacrifice. Even the exposition of the sacred Scriptures by the Son of God was not enough for these forlorn travelers. It was only when the bread was broken that they recognized the full presence of the risen Christ.

Christ is still with us. In the holy Sacrifice of the Mass, Catholic Christians believe that the eternal moment of Calvary is re-presented. Why? Because the blood shed on that holy hill knows no time and space. To all who will come to the foot of the cross, the crucified Savior offers mercy. The reality of his sacrifice is timeless and life-saving. We can partake of the precious gift of the Eucharist when we are tempted to avoid life's problems. In fact, attending daily Mass is a great source of strength for many Catholics in facing personal trials.

It is the passion of our Lord and Savior Jesus Christ—the complete offering of himself to the Father on our behalf on the rough wood of the cross—that represents the heart of the mystery of the gospel. In the wonderful words of St. Leo the Great:

> True reverence for the Lord's passion means fixing the eyes of our heart on Jesus crucified and recognizing in him our own humanity.

The earth—our earthly nature—should tremble at the suffering of its Redeemer. The rocks—the hearts of unbelievers—should burst asunder. The dead, imprisoned in the tombs of their mortality, should come forth, the massive stones now ripped apart. Foreshadowings of the future resurrection should appear in the holy city, the Church of God: what is to happen to our bodies should now take place in our hearts.[4]

Just as Jesus in his humanity did not avoid the cross because of his love not only for the Father, but for each one of us, so we must not avoid the cross of difficulty, struggle, and suffering in our own lives. For when that suffering is joined to the suffering of the divine Son of God, it is offered as a pure form of prayer and worship to the Father through him. Every time we are tempted to avoid some difficulty or pain in our lives, we can take it to the foot of the cross, either in the Sacrifice of the Mass or in personal prayer.

Like denial and control, avoidance—though seemingly easy—is ineffective and only makes matters worse. There are just some things in our life that won't go away. What really needs to change is us.

In fact, some of those things seem to hang around and haunt us. They are our own "thorns in the flesh" (2 Cor 12:7). They may be habit patterns or weaknesses of character that, if not properly handled, can become all consuming and self-destructive. Most tragically, they can lead us to sin. Moral theologians have often referred to weak areas in our lives and propensities to destructive patterns and sin as predominant faults.

Recognizing our own predominant faults takes honest admission, humility, and courage. But there is no other way. Each of us is called to imitate the passion of the Master. The question becomes: will those predominant faults lead to our self-destruction, or will they become clay in the Master's hands? The choice is ours.

Predominant Faults: Our Self-Destruction or Clay in the Master's Hands?

I T WAS AN ALL-TOO-FAMILIAR SCENE. An employee named Bernie who had been doing a very good job had asked to see me. It was shaping up to be a very busy day, and I did not expect to have any morning appointments. As he took his seat in my office, I could sense his apprehension. I tried to make him feel more comfortable.

"How can I help you, Bernie?" I asked.

"Well," he began, "this is very hard for me to say."

I tried to put his mind at ease and told him that I would welcome any suggestions he had. I wasn't prepared for the result.

"Well Keith," he said, "my problems are not with my job or our whole operation, my problems are with you. I have been hesitant to say anything. However, I just don't feel like you appreciate how hard I work," he said.

He detailed his experience of my functional approach to management. "I often feel like people are less important to you than accomplishing your goals," he concluded.

Well, Bernie's insights, as you know by now, hit the mark. All too often my approach to personal, family, and professional life has been to put a higher premium on accomplishing something than on fostering relationships.

After hearing Bernie out, I had a heart-to-heart discussion with him, acknowledging my weakness. But I also pointed out to him the importance of accomplishing my strategic objectives as a manager. He and I both left that candid conversation feeling better. I didn't promise Bernie that I would change tomorrow, but I did tell him I would work on it. And I am.

I believe that every one of us has vulnerable and weak areas in our emotional make-up and character that are very difficult to eliminate. Like buttons on a remote control device, they can launch us into unhealthy responses. If not curbed, they may lead us to destructive habits and lifestyles, possibly even serious sin and addictions. Moral theologians refer to these weaknesses or destructive patterns as predominant faults. What they show us is that we simply are not perfect. But as the bumper sticker says, "God Isn't Finished with Us Yet."

These buttons or predominant faults, however, can become the raw material out of which God's grace can fashion virtue and character. In a very real way, the choice is ours. An honest assessment and acknowledgment of our faults can make all the difference. Yet as we have seen earlier, we all too often respond to difficult things in the wrong way. Instead of honest admission and acknowledgment of our problems, we deny, try to control, and avoid them.

THE TWO PATHS AVAILABLE TO US

Two young men from similar backgrounds, whom I'll call John and Richard, are symbolic of the choice we all face. They also share common buttons or predominant faults. They stand as representatives of two roads: one which leads to health and holiness and the other which leads to denial and destruction.

In the Old Testament Book of Deuteronomy, we are presented with this fundamental choice in life:

Surely, this commandment that I am commanding you today is not too hard for you, nor is it too far away. It is not in heaven, that you should say, "Who will go up to heaven for us, and get it for us so that we may hear it and observe it?" Neither is it beyond the sea, that you should say, "Who will cross to the other side of the sea for us, and get it for us so that we may hear it and observe it?" No, the word is very near to you; it is in your mouth and in your heart for you to observe. See, I have set before you today life and prosperity, death and adversity. **Dt 30:11-14**

We must choose, and not just once, but many times every day. The Christian life is filled with choices, some seemingly small and insignificant and others life-changing. Following the Lord does not take choice away from us. Instead his Word, the direction and leadership of his church, and the Holy Spirit guide our decision-making so we can make informed choices. We are, in a very real and practical way, responsible for forming the consciences God has implanted in us, so we can make wise and prudent decisions. That is part of our dignity as children of God.

Let's take a look at the important issue of conscience formation before we turn to John and Richard. In the "Pastoral Constitution on the Church in the Modern World," the Fathers of the Second Vatican Council put it this way:

Deep within his conscience man discovers a law which he has not laid upon himself, but which he must obey. Its voice, ever calling into love and to do what is good and to avoid evil, tells him invariably at the right moment: do this, shun that... his conscience is man's most secret core, his sanctuary. There he is alone with God whose voice echoes in his depths. By conscience, in a wonderful way, that law is made known which is fulfilled in the love of God and of one's neighbor... hence the more a correct conscience prevails, the more do persons and groups turn aside from blind choice and try to be guided by the objective standards of moral conduct. **no. 16**

We are called to cultivate right judgment and then trust our consciences in the Lord, thereby directing our lives responsibly. But how can we form our consciences as Christians? There are reliable and objective sources through which God reveals his will to us. They include the sacred Scripture, natural law, and church teaching. Additionally, practicing Christian virtues both informs and transforms our lifestyles. But all of these are closely intertwined with our choices. John and Richard made different choices and, consequently followed very different roads.

John's grandfather was an alcoholic and as a result his family was, like many contemporary families, dysfunctional. As a young child he had faith in the Lord, but it waned in his teenage years. Then at college, he received a fresh touch of the Holy Spirit and was drawn back to his childhood faith. Strongly influenced by a campus evangelical group, he became an expert at quoting Scripture and learned to talk the contemporary "Christianese" of the circles in which he moved. He was attracted to those preaching what he called a "victorious gospel." His zeal soon developed an arrogant edge, however, so he alienated more people than he attracted to Christianity. Instead of engaging interested people in a meaningful dialogue about Christianity, he would parrot pat answers about everything, always including a Bible verse. Still John was convinced of his own spiritual maturity and mastery of the Christian life.

After graduation John began to experience the real world, and quickly became weighed down with the practical concerns of life and obsessed with his career. Eventually, he suffered a personal setback and succumbed to cocaine addiction. When his superficial piety could not explain adequately his craving for cocaine, he blamed God. He fell prey to a pattern of self-justification which often accompanies drug abuse and addiction.

When confronted with his drug use, John first denied he was addicted. "Half the adult population uses this stuff," he would respond. "I've got it under control." Then later, as the addiction worsened, he blamed it on others. "If they would just stop giving me this stuff, I'd stop using it," he would say. Finally, he wrongly blamed his father. "I grew up in a family of addicts," he would respond. "I guess this was all my father could pass on to me." Whenever a friend would confront John about his addiction, he simply told him, "Leave me alone." John was the child of someone who grew up in the 1960s, and it was bearing its bad fruit in a second generation.

John's father had used drugs recreationally for years. In fact, he smoked marijuana even as he was raising John. His son thus had a predisposition to using substances to avoid the tension and pressure that ordinary life brings. But now the substances were using John. His faith lacked depth upon which to draw. It drained away in a personal crisis, and John's bravado was overcome by unrelenting depression. John, with no room in his theology for suffering, could not reconcile his "prosperity gospel" with his struggle with drugs. Like the seed that fell among the thorns, his faith was soon choked away (Mt 13:6-7).

Richard, however, made very different choices. Raised in an alcoholic home, he too was well-acquainted with failure, struggle, and pain. Fortunately, Richard's father was a recovering alcoholic. He had openly shared with his children his own plight with this dreaded disease. He was actively involved in Alcoholics Anonymous and honest about his shortcomings.

In college, Richard grew closer to the Lord Jesus Christ and drew great inspiration from the lives of the saints. Like John, he received a fresh outpouring of the Spirit at a college prayer meeting, but his zeal for the Lord found a solid foundation in his love for his church and in an honest assessment of his own shortcomings. Because he had experienced honesty about failings in his own upbringing, Richard cultivated true humility in his own life. He also cultivated great mercy toward the failings of others. He was humble, not haughty, and won many to faith in Christ through his sincere life and compassionate heart.

As can happen though, even amidst great personal and spiritual growth, Richard began to experience a major problem— alcohol. Three years out of graduate school, Richard noted the growing influence that drinking was having in his life and the personality changes it was precipitating. One was a growing resentment and hostility toward his father. When he was fired from his first job, he went on an alcoholic binge.

Though it is not always the case, children of alcoholic parents are more likely to succumb to alcoholism. Statistics demonstrate that children of families with any significant addiction or serious dysfunction often repeat the family cycle.

In *Adult Children: The Secrets of Dysfunctional Families,* John and Linda Friel describe the characteristics of the downward spiral of addiction, which are indicative of Richard's experience:

1. preoccupation with the addictive agent;
2. increased tolerance for the addictive agent;
3. loss of control, where you can't have just one;
4. withdrawal, where you can't stop using whatever it is you're addicted to;
5. sneaking—such as hiding bottles and shamefully buying pornography and then hiding it in one's car;
6. denial—such as defensiveness about one's use of the addictive agent and one's symptoms;
7. personality changes and mood swings;
8. blaming, where it's everyone else's fault;
9. blackouts;
10. physical symptoms—headaches, ulcers, and the like;
11. rigid attitudes—black-and-white thinking and low tolerance of others' opinions;
12. loss of personal values, where you stop caring as the addiction progresses and don't take care of yourself;
13. disability or death—whether through physical damage due to a drug or chemical or through stress-related illnesses.[1]

Most authorities on addiction maintain that there is both a biological and emotional attachment to the substance involved. Richard had both. He kept his alcoholism a secret as long as he could. When his behavior began to change, he found himself operating by a set of rules that were like an old shoe, following the pattern his father had as an active alcoholic. Richard now needed to be in control of all interactions, feelings, and behavior. He always needed to be right about everything that he said or did. And he expected perfection not only from himself, but from others as well, whether at work or at home. When things didn't turn out the way he planned, he blamed others. It is not uncommon for those caught up in compulsive behavior to use blame in attempts to regain control. He also denied his own feelings and thoughts, drawing inward, and keeping everything to himself.

When he was confronted by friends and colleagues about the dramatic changes in his personality, he would deny them and reframe the entire issue. Richard was in total denial—denial of his addiction to alcohol and the gaping wound and emptiness inside. He was a miserable man. Further, the fact that Richard was taking on traits his father had before he went into recovery really scared Richard.

Ultimately, through the intervention of his father, Richard began attending a Twelve-Step group and received counseling to deal with what John Bradshaw often calls "the disease behind the disease"—the hole in his soul. Richard's deep emptiness inside, coupled with the genetic predisposition, needed serious attention.

Five years later, Richard is recovering from alcoholism and closer to the Lord than he was prior to hitting bottom. He is helping others both to meet Jesus Christ and to recover from their own addictions. He recognizes the need for recovery not only from chemical addictions, but compulsive behaviors. He now "boasts in his weakness" (2 Cor 12:5b), knowing that it is what keeps him close to the Lord. In fact, you will sometimes hear Richard in a moment of collegial prayer thank God for his alcoholism. When I first heard it, it sounded strange. But I soon came to understand the beauty of that expression of gratitude. Richard understood a deeper mystery of the kingdom of God—the link between God's redemptive plan and our pain. He is a man on the path to true holiness.

What is the difference between John and Richard? A lot. What is similar? More. Both are wounded and broken, with holes in their hearts and souls, desperately in need of a Savior.

Both have met that Savior. One, however, had no understanding in his faith for the inevitability and even value of suffering and fell prey to denial, control, and avoidance. The predominant fault of pride and arrogance got the upper hand. The other grasped the great mysteries and riches of the Christian faith. Through honest surrender and humility, he confronted his weakness.

HOW TO MINIMIZE OUR PREDOMINANT FAULTS

Suffering, woundedness, and brokenness are difficult paradoxes in the Christian life. Many of us, like John, blame God for our predominant faults and the resultant sufferings and difficulties. Subsequently, we fail to plumb the deeper message to be found in suffering and struggle. We attempt to rid ourselves of pain by ignoring it, denying it, or deadening it through an anesthetic such as alcohol, drugs, or food. It can even be bad spirituality. Honest admission of our faults is not only the road to recovery, but the way to true spirituality.

The apostle John, in his first letter to the early church, reminds us, "If we say that we have no sin, we deceive ourselves, and the truth is not in us. If we confess our sins, he who is faithful and just will forgive us our sins and cleanse us from all unrighteousness. If we say that we have not sinned, we make him a liar and his word is not in us" (1 Jn 1:8-10).

The principle is true not only about sin or an objective violation of the law of God, but also about weakness and failure. God knows what we are made of. He understands us better than we do ourselves. Yet we find it hard to accept his unconditional love. All too often, through our unwillingness to admit failings and faults, we undermine the grace that has been so freely offered to us.

The story of the prodigal son is one of the most powerful in the New Testament. It is an account of admission, repentance, and unconditional acceptance. After wasting his time, money, and talents on dissolute living, the prodigal finds himself caring for pigs on a farm and yearning to eat even the food the swine receive. Having hit bottom, the son honestly acknowledges his sinfulness and irresponsible lifestyle. He returns home prepared to repent, but before he can even get out the words, his merciful father sees him on the road. Running to meet his son, the father throws his arms around his neck and kisses him tenderly. The father's mercy and forgiveness are unconditional and total (Lk 15:11-32).

Hear the words of the father to his servants and apply them to God the Father's unconditional love for you in his Son Jesus, "'Quickly, bring out a robe—the best robe—and put it on him; put a ring on his finger and sandals on his feet. And get the fatted calf and kill it, and let us eat and celebrate; for this son of mine was dead and is alive again; he was lost and is found!'" (Lk 15:22).

That's what happens when we are honest about our plight as sinners, men and women with faults and weaknesses. We come alive again and find the way back home to our Father's house.

I don't know about you, but some of my predominant faults just don't seem to be going away anytime soon. I'm not talking about external circumstances that cause me grief, though they don't seem to be letting up either. I'm talking about the qualities that are so deeply ingrained in my nature and personality that I'd hardly recognize myself without them.

For example, I continue to struggle with my weight, although I am trim at the moment. I have been on absolutely every diet. I have been under spiritual obedience for it. I have discovered time and again what I had thought was the reason I continued to overeat. But I continue to be overweight much of the time. The most humbling thing about pounds is that you can't hide them. My weight is a barometer of my life. It is also a source of pain and a road to humility. It's not as if I haven't been trying to change. I have repented. I have confessed. I've read books. I've sought counsel from other Christians. With God's help, I have even won some victories. Still no matter what I do, some weaknesses refuse to budge. My progress hasn't been nearly as fast or steady as I'd have expected.

Much of my growth in the Lord, however, has involved minimizing the effects of weaknesses I've been unable to eliminate.

First, I've had to identify what they are, how they operate, and what triggers them. Then I try to surround myself with the environment and disciplines that can lessen their impact. For example, for me, working on some form of a Twelve-Step program to curb compulsive overeating is very helpful. Additionally, developing a daily regimen and getting support from my wife are very helpful. But compulsive overeating seems to be something that I can hold in check and not completely overcome.

I know you are probably thinking, "Aren't Christians supposed to be able to 'do all things through Christ who strengthens us'? Aren't we supposed to 'be perfect as our heavenly Father is perfect'?" You're right. Scripture also makes it clear that we will struggle from birth to death to become holy. In fact, the way of the cross is a slow process of what is traditionally called "white martyrdom." This is the daily suffering and sacrifice of self that does not result in the shedding of blood, but does result in the death of self-centeredness. In the words of the psalmist, "Precious in the sight of the Lord is the death of his faithful ones" (Ps 116:15).

When I finally reached the point where I realized I would never be perfect in this life, it was hard on me—perfectionist that I am. Somehow in our zeal for God, we can pick up the faulty notion that being baptized, committed, and faithful followers of Christ means that we shouldn't have struggles. Curiously, expecting perfection of ourselves can hold us back from becoming the man or woman God wants us to be. This is true because denying pain and difficulty won't make them go away. Owning them and taking responsibility for our behavior enables us to work through them so we are healthier.

I've come to believe that some of my weaknesses may take a long time to resolve, perhaps my whole life. This may sound like rationalization or lack of faith. I think, however, that it's a realistic assessment of my situation. Bravado will quickly fizzle when failure strikes. Cynicism, the other extreme, isn't a Christian response to problems. I have no intention of giving up on God's healing and saving power, but I have learned that time and patience are important elements of change.

It is discouraging to live with wounds that are slow to heal. "But," as C.S. Lewis wrote in *The Problem of Pain*, "pain insists upon being attended to." Like nothing else, it can rivet our attention and force us to deal with problems that we'd much rather ignore or give up on. Pain also gives us the humility to face our failings honestly and openly. We are utterly incapable of attaining the high ideals of the gospel without the unmerited grace and favor of God. If we're honest, our faults and weaknesses won't let us forget that.

OUR WOUNDS CAN BECOME REDEMPTIVE

Before you get too disheartened, let me share something else: our wounds, weaknesses, and struggles can become redemptive. God can manifest himself in our lives and work holiness into us through them. The pain we fear, the sin we hate, the weakness we're ashamed of—all can become agents of transformation in us. They can help us to move from pride and arrogance to humility. They help us identify with the weakness in others and become compassionate. They can help us learn to forgive and accept forgiveness, to love and accept love—perhaps for the first time.

St. Paul understood this. He defended himself before his Corinthian detractors by boasting about his weaknesses. He told them about his thorn in the flesh. He says that he even prayed three times that it might leave him. God did not answer Paul the way he would have liked. He said, "My grace is sufficient for you, for my power is made perfect in weakness" (2 Cor 12:9). God let the thorn remain, but only so it could instill holiness in his servant. Paul embraced the thorn, saying, "I will boast all the more gladly of my weaknesses, so that the power of Christ may dwell in me. Therefore I am content with weaknesses, insults, hardships, persecutions, and calamities for the sake of Christ; for whenever I am weak, then I am strong" (2 Cor 12:9-10).

Paul learned, as we must learn, that a mature Christian

doesn't have everything going perfectly in his life. A mature Christian embraces his or her weaknesses and allows God to use them to make him or her "perfect as our heavenly Father is perfect." One doesn't give up trying to rid oneself of sin and weaknesses, but instead gives up anything that would prevent one from moving on in the Lord.

I was glad when I at last gave up a false idea of perfection in this earthly life. A commentary on Matthew 5:48, the verse about being perfect as the Father is perfect, set me straight on this. The commentator points out that the Greek word for perfect refers to the *potential* of a person or thing to grow, develop, and become mature or complete. He adds: "Mature, complete Christians persevere in trials and count them as joy because they believe that God desires only what is truly best for them. Mature Christians take on the qualities of Christ, but are not controlled or grieved by the past, and they view the future with hope. Mature Christians realize that there is a reorganization going on in them of behaviors and values and lifestyle and self-perceptions, and they desire to become like Christ, yet they are aware of their progress without a sense of failure or arrival. Not really too concerned with either; concerned mostly with faithfulness."[2]

When we think of being perfect as never doing anything to displease God or hurt our brothers and sisters, it becomes an unattainable ideal. Viewing perfection as an ongoing process that will finally yield completeness or maturity not only is manageable, but consistent with reality. If we see our struggles as moving us toward a long-term goal, rather than as daily evidence of our failure to achieve that goal, we can experience more peace, joy, and confidence in our spiritual growth.

Another thing that's helped me appreciate the work God is doing in me is meditating on the wounds of Jesus Christ crucified. Those wounds purchased my freedom from sin and death and brought me salvation. They are precious to me. They must be precious to the Father as well, because those wounds are still present in Jesus' resurrected body. They are a testimony to the great price the Son of God paid for our salvation.

WILL OUR GLORIFIED BODIES BEAR OUR WOUNDS?

I've often wondered if our wounds will remain in our glorified bodies. Usually I think of a glorified body as one of surpassing beauty and perfection. But the only resurrected body anyone has ever seen has nail prints in the hands and feet and a lance-pierced side. If Jesus' body still bears the marks of his suffering, is it not reasonable to suppose that our bodies may bear the marks of our suffering as well? Whether physical, emotional, or spiritual, our sufferings and struggles, when joined to Christ, are precious and productive.

I don't mean to suggest that our resurrected bodies will experience pain, but that our wounds will be visible, as Jesus' are, as evidence of the love God has for us. In his glorified body, Jesus' wounds brought his disciples joy and faith, not sorrow and fear. "He showed them his hands and his side. Then the disciples rejoiced when they saw the Lord" (Jn 20:20). When Jesus told Thomas to examine his wounded hands and side, Thomas responded, "My Lord and my God!" (Jn 20:28). Imagine the healing that this affirmation of faith accomplished in Thomas' doubting heart and mind!

Perhaps in heaven we will perceive our wounds as beautiful, because they will make it clear just how much of Christ's redeeming, healing, and restorative grace it took to bring us into his eternal kingdom. Remember what Jesus tells Simon the Pharisee about the woman who washed his feet with her tears, "Therefore, I tell you, her sins, which were many, have been forgiven; hence she has shown great love. But the one to whom little is forgiven, loves little" (Lk 7:47).

Have you ever wondered what you will look like in your resurrected body? Obviously all we can do is speculate, but I sincerely wonder if our idea of full redemption is accurate. I realized that when I thought of the resurrected body, I thought of some pristine image that was too aesthetically brilliant for the human eye. Perhaps we will look like that, but do we leave room for the possibility of the resurrection being nothing like what we might imagine? After all, St. Paul tells us that "what no eye has seen, nor ear heard, nor the human heart conceived, what God has prepared for those who love him" (1 Cor 2:9). I wonder if our concept of glorification and perfection are so desperately in need of redemption that when we are before him and we see him as he is, our whole understanding will change. You see, the issue cuts much deeper than simply the appearance of glorified bodies with wounds. It cuts to the heart of our conception of redemption and sanctification.

Wasn't the primary reason for Christ's wounds to pay the penalty for our salvation? He was broken that we might be healed. He took upon himself the woundedness of us all, became bruised for the penalty of our sin, and we now have the gift of eternal fellowship with God through him. His life and his death have thus become the pattern for our own, a reality which is reflected in our common baptism into Christ. So we cherish the wounds of Christ because they have purchased our freedom.

Perhaps our wounds are going to become personal treasures because they have helped us become more like Jesus. They will have helped us grow in holiness. They will have helped us to move from pride and arrogance to humility. They will have helped us become compassionate and empathetic with the weak and wounded. They will have enabled us to grow in being able to forgive and love as Jesus forgave and loved. Our woundedness can do this!

After all, we can empathize with the pain of others when we ourselves have experienced pain at a deep level. It is no longer something we have just read or speculated about. Rather, it is something that we know deep in our gut. My own continual struggle with weight has made me a lot more tolerant of those who are not able to overcome personal weakness. My own experience of failure has made me less demanding of perfection in others.

THE VALUE OF PAIN

When Paul wrote to the Corinthians, he was responding to people who were questioning his apostolic authority. Interestingly, Paul defended himself on the basis of his own weaknesses. He talked to the Corinthians about his handwriting and how frail it was, about his physical weaknesses, about his thorn in the flesh and his struggles. Yes, St. Paul pleaded with the Lord to take away his thorn. There is absolutely nothing wrong with asking the Lord to take away pain. But God did not answer Paul the way he in his humanness would have liked. God chose a bigger "yes" for Paul. He said, "My grace is sufficient for you, for power is made perfect in weakness" (2 Cor 12:9).

Paul boasts not about his spiritual revelations or his special call—but rather about his sufferings, his struggles, his being left for dead, his being misunderstood, his burden for the churches he shepherded, his wounds—in short, his many difficulties and the incredible grace of God that sustained him.

St. Teresa of Avila often prayed to be the Lord's hands and feet. I have reflected on this many times, and each time I get a similar thought. The hands and feet of Jesus were wounded. If we desire to be transformed into his image, we need to ask ourselves what it means to have wounded feet, wounded hands, a bleeding head, or a pierced side. All of us have known the ache of pain, but the pain itself is not purifying. Purification and transformation come to the degree that we choose to unite our wounds with Christ and begin to become more like him.

How does this happen? God allows us thorns in the flesh, but as with Paul, he can transform our very thorns into vehicles of holiness. Embracing our very woundedness can be a powerful step toward full redemption. Until we reach that final day, we are seeking continual, dynamic transformation in Christ— to become more like him every day, to be transformed from glory to glory (2 Cor 3).

In 1 John we read, "What we will be has not yet been revealed. What we do know is this: when he is revealed, we will be like him, for we will see him as he is" (1 Jn 3:2). If we are being transformed from glory to glory, then we are beginning to look, act, and react more like Christ. If we continue on earth to move and grow daily in God's presence, we are, in a certain sense, going to be like God. That is overwhelming. We're not there yet, but the only way we can get there is through this inner transformation and purification—a dynamic process that more often than not occurs through struggle and difficulty, weakness and frailty.

If we don't have any room in our theology for this kind of redemptive suffering, for this approach to dealing with weakness and predominant faults, we may become confused and disappointed in our spiritual journey. Worse, we may become hardhearted and cynical because problems and struggles continue. Instead of expecting or waiting for our pain to vanish, we need to change our response and examine the root issues— the heart of the matter.

When we begin to understand this mystery, we begin to discern the difference between a weakness, fault, or struggle that can be changed, and a struggle that may continue for years. Such discernment can only develop over time if our traveling companion is the Lord Jesus.

Many of us are naive about what it means to call upon God's power. We may say, "I can do all things through [Christ] who strengthens me" (Phil 4:13). I can do *all things*—what does that really mean? We may even pretend that we don't experience or shouldn't experience problems as Christians. This was John's approach to cocaine addiction, but it fell short and so did John. Victory in Jesus does not mean we sail through life trouble-free. It means that we call upon God's strength, wisdom, and power to raise us up through struggles and even to allow struggle to become the very thing about our lives that most glorifies our Father.

When we deny, avoid, or try to control problems, most likely those same problems will resurface in another form. Christians especially are ashamed to admit struggle, but just because we are baptized, committed, and faithful followers of Christ does not mean our struggles will disappear. We should be positive, however, and focus on the fact that we are new creations in Christ (2 Cor 5:17) and can daily be recreated in his image. We have changed internally, what we value has changed, and what we hold on to and treasure has changed. Shouldn't then our way of viewing problems change as well?

Another mistake is to nurture a defeatist attitude. We may say, "I can't do anything about my weakness. That's just the way I am. And people should accept me the way I am." It is true that we all have a God-given personality. It is also true that God's grace can cultivate our natural character. Therefore, through our response to God's power, we can bring under submission to him unhealthy patterns that block his healing. But our response is key. We need to own both our strengths *and* weaknesses and take responsibility for our behavior. When we take *ownership* of our problems, we learn how to work through them in a healthy way.

OUR COMPLETION IN CHRIST—OWNERSHIP

Psychologist James Fowler, in his book *Stages of Faith*, discusses progress in personal maturity. In his view, we need to move toward the stage of ownership, or becoming personally responsible for our lives. This is true in our walk of faith. It is true of spiritual maturity. We need to acknowledge our responsibility for our successes and our failures while avoiding the trap of perfectionism. We are simply hoping to become more like Jesus. The actual word used for perfection in the passage from Matthew 5:4-7 is *telios*, which is more accurately rendered "complete." Something is *telios* when it has completed the purpose for which it was designed. We were made for God. He will have us in the end. He has prepared our road to that ultimate union.

The apostle James tells us: "Whenever you face trials of any kind, consider it nothing but joy" (Jas 1:2). Complete Christians persevere in trials and count them as pure joy because they believe that God desires for them only what is best. Complete Christians are not controlled by the past. They view the future with hope. Complete Christians realize that God is engaged with a total reorganization of their behavior patterns, responses, values, lifestyles, and self-perceptions—all because God is faithful in granting their desire to become like Christ and all in his good time. Even though these Christians experience continual change, they view their progress without a sense of failure or arrival. They are concerned more with fidelity than some self-imposed goal. After all, our sense of timing and the Lord's are often, literally, light years away. As Psalm 90 tells us, "For a thousand years in your sight are like yesterday when it is past, or like a watch in the night" (v. 4).

Dealing with illness, weakness, and struggles is challenging, but God can give us resiliency. We experience true freedom when we embrace what is closest to our hearts. I embrace being a Catholic Christian. I embrace being in relationship with Jesus Christ. I am weak and frail; but by the grace of Christ Jesus, I am, *through* my weakness, being transformed into his image. I no longer run from or try to deny my struggles. Rather, I seek to embrace them joyfully as God's gifts to help me become more like him. This is not the easy way, but the way of the cross. No one ever said it would be easy. Especially Jesus.

Maybe when the last trumpet sounds, millions upon millions of glorified bodies will come forth from their tombs adorned with glorified wounds—wounds that, when joined with the five wounds of the Son of God, are seen as the very agents that made possible their owners' earthly transformation. Whatever our predominant faults or buttons may be, some of them may then be worn with gratitude because they broke us of the greatest impediment to contentment, false pride.

So many of us have been affected deeply by the ills of this present age. Dysfunctional families in a dysfunctional society strap us with limitations which we are either unaware of or unable to handle. When the bottom falls out of our boxed universe, we fall through. But when we fall out of our boxed universe, the arms of a loving God are there to catch us.

Our predominant faults are guarantees of our continuing need for a Savior. When honestly acknowledged, they can become an open door to his transforming grace, one day at a time. They can help us take personal responsibility for our lives, so we can begin to enjoy the spiritual freedom of sons and daughters of God.

6 | Taking Personal Responsibility

What's Wrong with the World?
—London Times
I am... —G.K. Chesterton

I COULD TELL FROM MY FATHER'S raised eyebrows that I was in deep trouble. So I looked over at my mother hoping that I would be able to escape his wrath. But she looked just as angry. "Why did you kick your brother?" my father screamed. In the meantime my brother, Stephen, was in tears. He had tattled on me again. I was so frustrated with him that I had just hauled off and kicked him right in the derriere. But what's a seven-year-old to do in a situation like this?

"I didn't do it," I said.

"What do you mean you didn't do it, Keith?" cried my mother. "Are you saying that Stephen lied?"

The screams of my brother then began to drown me out. "You did too! You did too! You did too, do it! You kicked me."

"Well, young man," opined my father, "what do you have to say for yourself now?"

"I didn't do it," I insisted stubbornly. *"My foot slipped!"*

It sounds humorous now, doesn't it? But it revealed an approach to life that was already taking root within me as a young boy. I didn't want to take responsibility because I did not want to face the consequences. So I didn't kick my brother, my foot just slipped. With five children of my own now, I see how humorous it must have been. But my parents kept a straight face. They didn't buy the excuse. G.K. Chesterton wouldn't have bought it either.

In an editorial, the *London Times* raised the question "What's Wrong with the World?" It invited its readers to respond. An overwhelming number did. Among them was G.K. Chesterton, one of the great Christian writers and thinkers of this century. Out of all the letters his was the shortest, the simplest, and the most on target. In response to the question, "What's Wrong with the World?" G.K. Chesterton wrote, "*I am.*" And you know what? He was right. So am I. So are you. So are we all.

It took me a long time to appreciate the profound understanding of sin and personal responsibility behind Chesterton's remark. Summed up in those two words is a fundamental truth about the human condition as well as a Christian premise. It has been grasped by great Christian men and women throughout the ages. St. Paul wrote to his disciple, Timothy: "The saying is sure and worthy of full acceptance: Christ Jesus came into the world to save sinners—*of whom I am the foremost.* But for that very reason I received mercy, so that in me, as the foremost of sinners, Christ Jesus might display the utmost patience, making me an example to those who would come to believe in him for eternal life. Now to the King of the ages, immortal, invisible, the only God, be honor and glory forever and ever. Amen" (1 Tm 1:15-17, emphasis mine).

In that letter and throughout his writings, Paul reveals his thorough grasp of this fundamental truth, confessing his sinfulness before God. His declarations are not expressions of piety of the moment, nor are they lamentations of one with a bad self-image. An exaggerated sense of shame can become toxic and can lead people to believe they are worthless. But St. Paul knew his worth. In fact, "he boasted in the Lord," and he "boasted in his weakness" (2 Cor 11:30). He knew who he was and who God was for him. He was a self-assured man. Paul had found the secret to true freedom. He owned responsibility for his personal sins and his shared responsibility for the corporate sins of his age. He also believed in the unconditional, unmerited love and mercy of God. That is what grace is all about. We cannot forgive our own sins or earn God's favor.

THE TRAP OF LEGALISM

When we subscribe to legalism, we lose the freedom given us through grace.[1] Legalism is an attempt to please God through our effort or works. It is subtle and insidious. It offers a counterfeit freedom. And falling back into legalism is a danger for every Christian. It has been a threat to the Christian church from its very beginnings. The church of Galatia is an excellent example. A vibrant community founded by Paul, the apostle of grace, it fell prey to the Judaizers, a group of early Christians who taught that re-embracing the complete law was the only vehicle to salvation. Paul had to correct the Galatians and remind them that they had received grace freely.

The Galatian error is still with us. Sidney was a part of a small church in a large metropolitan area. Initially, the church gathered together to worship, and then members of the congregation began to pool their resources in a local outreach to inner city residents. As the ministry of the church grew, so did the desire for stability and greater unity. Soon members began to meet once a week to make decisions about their outreach. For five years, the church and its outreach flourished.

Yet differences between church members began to become increasingly evident. Since they came from all over a large metropolitan area, their lifestyle approaches, their entertainment decisions, even their style of dress at church services and meetings were too dissimilar. They also wanted to provide an alternative culture to the inner city residents they served.

Thus, the decision was made to develop some overall approaches to things like dress, lifestyle, and family life. Within several years, the church was no longer flourishing and its customs had evolved into rigid rules. Members dressed and spoke a certain way and began to expect new members to act the same way. The emphasis had shifted from loving and accepting others and bringing them into maturity in Christ to following a set of rules that reinforced the common culture.

Sidney knew that it was time to leave. It was the words of St. Paul to the Galatians that leaped off the page during his devotions one morning: "You foolish Galatians! Who has bewitched you? It was before your eyes that Jesus Christ was publicly exhibited as crucified. The only thing I want to learn from you is this: Did you receive the Spirit by doing the works of the law or by believing what you heard? Are you so foolish? Having started with the Spirit, are you now ending with the flesh?" (Gal 3:1-3). Sidney's experience is not uncommon.

This kind of legalism, or trying to earn God's favor, brings "the treadmill curse." "Those who labor under legalism walk around with a gnawing in their gut that says, 'Whatever you do, it's not enough....'"[2] We are called to walk in grace and to continually acknowledge our powerlessness, need for God, and responsibility for sin, if we are to find forgiveness and freedom. The Twelve Steps keep me returning to the foot of the cross of Calvary. There God demonstrated unmerited favor to the world. The cross is a scandal to those who seek to earn their own righteousness. But to those of us who have felt the awesome love of God, it is the place of human liberation.

John Paul II continually reminds us that we are "unique and unrepeatable human beings." We have been given free will. No one can substitute an act of his or her will for our own. We are responsible for our own acts. I am responsible for my acts. I am responsible for my choices. I am responsible for my failures. I am responsible for my relationship with the Lord and others. Personalizing and owning our thoughts and deeds is critical to our human maturity. Yet it is all too often not our experience. Instead, we can play the blame game, or drive ourselves to perform.

Pastor Ken Wilson puts it this way: "Legalism appeals to something in us... the flesh. We would like to please God by human effort. Then we have ourselves to be proud of. Who wouldn't like to stand before the Judgment Seat and say, 'I did it! You got me started, but then I ran a good race! I prayed every day, took care of all my responsibilities, did everything required of me. I made it [with your help, of course].' That appeals to the flesh. Legalism—oddly enough—appeals to our desperate need for acceptance. Don't we all have a desperate need for acceptance? Wouldn't we go anywhere, do anything for acceptance? This thirst for acceptance is as powerful as the thirst for water."[3]

ACKNOWLEDGMENT OF OUR RESPONSIBILITY

The way to acceptance is not by attempting to earn God's favor. The way to acceptance is by amazing grace, by owning and acknowledging responsibility for our sins and walking in freedom. It sounds so easy, doesn't it? But if you are like me, it is very difficult. The acknowledgment I am talking about is not mere lip service, but must come from the heart. In biblical terms, the heart is the center of a person, the place where the person makes his or her most fundamental decisions. This is the place where grace must find a home.

A cartoon which appeared in a popular Christian magazine depicted a psychiatrist with a moustache and pince-nez glasses sitting behind a large desk. Seated in front of him was a miserable-looking, disheveled fellow who was asking the shrink, "Take responsibility for my own life? Is that legal?"

It is not only legal, it is essential to personal and spiritual growth. It's the road to *true* perfection, meaning completion. And it is often the missing element in our lives. Responsibility is simply a matter of being honest with ourselves and with God.

Melody Beattie writes, "Before I began recovery, the concept of being honest with anyone, including myself, never occurred to me. From the time I was old enough to talk, being honest about who I was, and what I thought, felt, believed, wanted, and didn't want, was out of the question. I had no *honesty training*"[4] (emphasis mine).

Many of us have not had honesty training, yet honesty is at

the heart of conversion, recovery, and renewal. Step Five of every recovery process challenges the person to "admit to God, to oneself, and to another human being the nature of our wrongs." Such admission results in inner honesty and is basic to conversion of the heart. Such admission leads to forgiveness and freedom from past hurts.

OWNING AND PERSONALIZING OUR RESPONSIBILITY

Every significant point of my conversion has been directly related to a deeper level of honesty, ownership, and personalization. On a beach in Santa Cruz, California, when I knelt down and gave my life back to Jesus Christ, I finally owned my responsibility for what was wrong with my world. I was. This act opened the door to the one who stands at the door of every human heart and knocks. Hear the words of Jesus himself: "Listen! I am standing at the door, knocking; if you hear my voice and open the door, I will come in to you and eat with you, and you with me" (Rv 3:20).

These words, taken from the Book of Revelation, are addressed to the church in Laodicea, whose believers had become lukewarm. In short, they had become reliant upon themselves: "You say, 'I am rich, I have prospered, and I need nothing.' You do not realize that you are wretched, pitiable, poor, blind, and naked. Therefore I counsel you to buy from me gold refined by fire so that you may be rich; and white robes to clothe you and to keep the shame of your nakedness from being seen; and salve to anoint your eyes so you may see. I reprove and discipline those whom I love. Be earnest, therefore, and repent" (Rv 3:17-19).

We too can become smug and self-sufficient. Sometimes that is merely a cover for a lack of confidence in ourselves and God. Or perhaps we sense something is wrong, but we try to deaden our consciences because we don't want to face the pain of changing.

In my own life, after years of teenage rebellion spent pointing the finger of blame at everybody else, it finally pointed back at me. I could no longer pass the buck. I was the problem.

The apostle James gives us a profound answer to an often-asked question: "Those conflicts and disputes among you, where do they come from? Do they not come from your cravings that are at war within you? You want something and do not have it; so you commit murder. And you covet something and cannot obtain it; so you engage in disputes and conflicts. You do not have because you do not ask" (Jas 4:1-2).

At a very early age, I thought I saw the world's problems clearly. I wanted to solve them. I eagerly applied myself to this challenge. I wanted to become an agent of change. I marched on Washington, D.C., to protest the Vietnam War. I edited an underground newspaper which took on the system. I sought to raise the consciousness of people about the plight of those trapped in an endless cycle of poverty. I fervently joined in the counterculture of the 1960s and 1970s, hoping to change what I saw as a self-centered, materialistic society. I still disagree with some of the political approaches of that day and still believe that the rebellion and anger I felt were rooted in a rightful rejection of global self-centeredness. But the problem was that the solutions being offered were worse than that self-centeredness. Let me illustrate.

My friend, David, and I attended a rally of hundreds of thousands of anti-war demonstrators at the Washington Memorial in our nation's capitol. We were filled with youthful idealism. It was at the height of the anti-war demonstrations against United States involvement in Vietnam. I remember that we raised our hands in unison, flashing the peace sign, and singing, "All we are saying is give peace a chance." Euphoria filled the air.

In the distant background I could hear a chant. At first I thought it was the crowd far away catching up with our chant "... is give peace a chance." I was wrong. A group of other demonstrators began to get closer and closer, working their way through the crowd. When I finally made them out in the distance, I saw they were carrying the flag of the National Liberation Front, the Communist Viet Cong Army—the actual enemies of American soldiers risking their lives in the muddy rice paddies of Vietnam. They were chanting, "Ho- Ho- Ho-Chi-Minh, N.L.F. is gonna win!"

I couldn't believe my ears. Was that what this assembly was about? That wasn't my intention! Nor was it the intention of the vast majority of my fellow demonstrators. "But what is our solution?" I asked myself. "How can we stop the killing?"

Suddenly I doubted my participation in the demonstration. "Keith," I asked myself, "what are you doing here? Is this really going to end the war? Are you being used?" Within minutes, panic swept through the crowd. The protesters had thrown red paint all over the Justice Department Building across the street. Windows had been smashed. The crowd was reacting to news of the "trashing of the Justice Department Building."

Soon riot police on horseback charged into the crowd. All around me people were being struck and injured. Many had fallen to the ground, knocked down by riot police or reacting to the tear gas that had been released to disperse the crowd.

Here I was, a fifteen-year-old idealistic kid with all hell breaking loose around me. Choking and gasping for breath, I ran from the tear gas along with David. I avoided physical injury, but I would never be the same on the inside.

On returning home, I quickly became apolitical. I realized that my efforts to overcome injustice in the world were not bearing fruit. The system that I railed against wasn't the only problem. There were competing systems and agendas offered as alternatives, and none of them seemed to hold the solution either.

Shortly after that chilling experience, I threw myself into the study of religious writings. I read the *Upanishads, The Bhagavad Gita,* and other Hindu scriptures. I studied other exotic spiritualities as well. But I kept returning to the Bible. I was looking for the answer to what was wrong with the world.

I had hung out with others who were rejecting the system. What I had found out, however, was that the same system existed in their midst—a system of self-centeredness, a system of greed. They only used different words. I was also beginning to see that the same system existed inside of me. But I had yet to own my responsibility for what was happening around me.

That personalization and ownership came later with my conversion. I finally realized that all that I saw that was wrong around me was wrong inside me.

It's interesting to note that all the post-resurrection accounts of Jesus demonstrate ownership and personalization on behalf of the disciples, all of whom doubted that he would fulfill his promises. They also doubted that he was really alive (Mk 16:9-14; Lk 24; Jn 20).

Once again, it is the beloved disciple, John, who sets forth for us one of the most wonderful accounts of ownership and personalization by the apostle Thomas.

> But Thomas (who was called the Twin), one of the twelve, was not with them when Jesus came. So the other disciples told him, "We have seen the Lord." But he said to them, "Unless I see the mark of the nails in his hands, and put my finger in the mark of the nails and my hand in his side, I will not believe."
>
> A week later his disciples were again in the house, and Thomas was with them. Although the doors were shut, Jesus came and stood among them and said, "Peace be with you." Then he said to Thomas, "Put your finger here and see my hands. Reach out your hand and put it in my side. Do not doubt but believe." Thomas answered him, "My Lord and my God!" Jesus said to him, "Have you believed because you have seen me? Blessed are those who have not seen and yet come to believe." **Jn 20:24-29**

Thomas heard the words of the risen Christ and responded in faith. He had heard the account of his brothers and sisters. But he had not owned his belief in the resurrection. In fact, it would take probing the wounds of Christ himself to bring Thomas to a personalized faith.

My own spiritual journey didn't end that day on the beach when I experienced conversion. It only began. It soon led me back to the early church and the apostles. Then I journeyed through twenty centuries of Christian history, struggling with each article of the profession of faith, "The Apostle's Creed."

I believe in God, the Father almighty, creator of heaven and earth; And in Jesus Christ, his only Son, our Lord; who was conceived by the Holy Spirit, born of the Virgin Mary, suffered under Pontius Pilate, was crucified, died, and was buried. He descended into hell; the third day he arose again from the dead; He ascended into heaven, and sits at the right hand of God, the Father almighty; from thence He shall come to judge the living and the dead. I believe in the Holy Spirit, the holy catholic Church, the communion of saints, the forgiveness of sins, the resurrection of the body, and life everlasting. Amen.

I have seen time and again how important it is to personalize and own my faith. But like many important truths, this one is like jello—hard to hold on to. It must be rediscovered again and again.

Many years later I had the privilege of serving on the staff of the Franciscan University of Steubenville,[5] where I wore several hats successively: general counsel, presidential assistant, dean of evangelism, and dean of students.

As dean of students, I was responsible for the overall way of life of the student body. I threw myself into the job with zeal for the Lord, which was also symptomatic of my tendency to fall into the trap of performance. I wanted to see these young men and women, whose hearts were so alive, fully embrace the teachings of the church and the Scriptures. I was attempting to integrate into a transient student environment, the principles of commitment and community. The student-life model on the campus of Franciscan University were "faith households."

As mentioned in chapter one, under the direction of the college president, Fr. Michael Scanlan, I began the first faith household. It pioneered a unique approach to student living. Ten to fifteen students in a wing of a dormitory had the opportunity to develop a vibrant life together, sharing prayer, Scripture study, the sacraments, and daily life as brothers and sisters in Christ.

However, in attempting to oversee this pastoral model, I was shocked to run into a myriad of discipline problems. Though these existed when I was a student, I supposed they had gone away as the campus matured. But I now know that they are typical of all college campuses, and very typical of teenagers in general.

My naiveté combined with my inability to help the students really change led me to an intense study of how people do change. I began to read the books of developmental theorists, such as Piaget and Fowler. They deepened my understanding of the nature of conversion and change. Consistent themes began to emerge from their work. I began to understand that human development and spiritual maturity require struggle and even doubt, which then gives birth to ownership. The process of taking personal responsibility for one's life does not happen overnight.

On that journey toward maturity, the finger that blames everyone but oneself will turn about and point back at us. I'm grateful for that experience. It helped prepare me for raising my own teenage daughter. Though I do not parent perfectly, I know I handle it better than I would have back then. Even more, it gave me a more realistic view of myself and others.

LIFELONG CONVERSION

Only over time have I come to understand more deeply that the process of change and conversion never ends. Everyone's life is in process. We are "putting off the old and putting on the new" (2 Cor 5:17). Paul reminded the Colossians:

> But now you must get rid of all such things—anger, wrath, malice, slander, and abusive language from your mouth. Do not lie to one another, seeing that you have stripped off the old self with its practices and have clothed yourselves with the new self, which is being renewed in knowledge according to the image of its creator....
>
> As God's chosen ones, holy and beloved, clothe your-

selves with compassion, kindness, humility, meekness, and patience. Bear with one another and, if anyone has a complaint against another, forgive each other; just as the Lord has forgiven you, so you also must forgive. Above all, clothe yourselves with love, which binds everything together in perfect harmony. And let the peace of Christ rule in your hearts, to which indeed you were called in the one body.

Col 3:8-15

This process of taking off the old manner of living and putting on the new is a lifetime affair. We make progress, then fall back and begin again. That is why it is a life of recovery and renewal. In recovery circles, the process of going back through the same pattern that we thought we had overcome is often referred to as "recycling."[6] A story is told about an encounter between a recovering person and one who was seeking recovery. "Tell me about the reality of recovery," one said. "Oh that," the other replied. "You mean two steps forward and one step back." That's what the life of renewal is all about as well. But progress is steady if we persevere.

As mentioned earlier, a criticism of integrating the Twelve-Step process and Christian spirituality is that the steps encourage people to point the finger of blame at others. Sometimes this charge has merit. Many people do get stuck in the steps. And we do indeed live in a blame-oriented society. However, establishing blame is not the goal of the Twelve-Step process. Rather, it is designed to be a practical approach for people to take responsibility for their lives. If approached in the right way, it facilitates ownership and personalization, moving the individual from blame to responsibility. It also helps people overcome low self-esteem, another significant roadblock on the path to spiritual maturity.

There is danger in any process. Religion itself can be misused. Remember the words of Karl Marx, "Religion is the opiate of the masses." Unfortunately, many seemingly religious people in his day had allowed their piety to degenerate into mere external acts, which lent credibility to Marx's criticisms.

THE DEAD END OF TOXIC SHAME AND SCRUPULOSITY

The necessity of having healthy self-esteem while growing in a knowledge of our own sinfulness and responsibility is critical, but often misunderstood. Set against that balance is toxic shame and scrupulosity.

The market is flooded today with books on how to improve our lives. Many of them do help. However, often their readers don't accept their own frailty, weakness, and powerlessness. In other words, they are people who don't accept the messiness of life. Many of them, like myself, struggle with toxic shame and an accompanying lack of self-worth.

Many times I have buried my fear of failure, insecurity, and lack of confidence behind a show of bravado. But deep inside I was—and at times, am—ashamed of myself because I am the product of shaming.

As I've stressed before, I have tremendous love for my father. He, like every other human being, carries with him his past. Orphaned at a very early age, he spent most of his childhood in a boarding school. As a result, he had no real experience of fathering. He did the best he could and I love him deeply for that. However, my love for him has not come easily.

Probably because he had to fight for everything he got, my father's approach to life and childrearing caused long-term difficulties in me. It also produced a cycle that, with the help of God, I am trying to break in rearing my own children. My father and I are very impatient and intolerant men. By God's grace, I am working on it.

I remember as a child regularly experiencing the brunt of these qualities in my father. His opinion of me and my behavior was often revealed in harsh words and facial expressions. It continues to amaze me when I think of the impact expressions like, "All right, young man..." had on me. I always cringed and knew that when he called me "young man," what followed was going to hurt. Then there were the eyebrows. By simply moving his eyebrows, my father could make me feel ashamed and afraid. Worse than the eyebrows, were the eye rolls—the signal that he was about to get angry. Right before he went over the edge, his bottom jaw would jut out, his eyebrows would arch, and his eyes would roll. Then I knew, I had really crossed him.

Unfortunately, I have inherited the eyebrows. I regularly have to work on how I use them with my own children. The facial expressions of my father were symptomatic of his shaming approach to childrearing. The result was a deep hole in my soul. I am not blaming my father; I love him. I'm pointing to a very real lack of affirmation in my home. As a result, I developed an external toughness and learned, at a very early age, to take charge. I projected an aura of confidence which throughout my entire adult life has been misconstrued by friends and colleagues, who did not see that deep inside I was hungering for affirmation.

And so do we all. When was the last time you said to your spouse, child, or colleague, "You are good," or "You are beautiful," or "You've done a wonderful job"? I know that these affirming expressions come all too rarely from my lips, but with the help of God, I am working on being more supportive.

Jesus knew the importance of affirmation. We have seen that Jesus knew what Peter was made of, yet knowing all of this, Jesus said to Peter, "And I tell you, you are Peter, and on this rock I will build my church" (Mt 16:18). He did not belittle Peter when Peter made mistakes. He reinforced in Peter a sense of self-worth.

Throughout the Bible, we find God changing the names of those whom he calls. Abram becomes Abraham. Jacob becomes Israel. Simon becomes Peter. Saul becomes Paul. In the Bible a name means a great deal. It captures the identity of a person. That is what God does in each of us. He reveals our identity to us as we cooperate with his grace. No matter how deficient our upbringing, God our Father can make up for it all through the revelation of his perfect love in Jesus Christ. "God is love, and those who abide in love abide in God, and God abides in them" (1 Jn 4:16). Yet the overwhelming majority of us have a deep "love hunger."[7]

Unfortunately, a lot of Christians bear toxic shame because

of their upbringing. While they need to ground their identities in Christ as new creations, even their church can become an extended dysfunctional family characterized by toxic shame. It doesn't have to be that way. One key is understanding the distinction between healthy and unhealthy shame.

Healthy shame is the good fruit of a well-formed conscience responding to objective wrongdoing. The person acknowledges his or her responsibility for such behavior. Since sin is involved, he or she seeks repentance and restitution. Healthy shame focuses on the *behavior,* whereas toxic shame focuses instead on the *person,* making the person "bad" or shameful. Toxic shame is a terrible enemy to growth, freedom, and a good self-image. Many times it produces the bad fruit of scrupulosity.

Great spiritual writers over the ages have identified scrupulosity as a very dangerous spiritual problem. Scrupulous people see themselves as totally flawed and unworthy. They have embraced toxic shame to the point where they are no longer people with problems, but they themselves have become the problem. Scrupulosity is the spiritualizing of a bad self-image.

Unfortunately, scrupulosity and its accompanying poor self-image can dress itself up in spiritual terms, such as sham piety that, at first glance, may appear to be genuine. I have seen groups with such scrupulosity. It is a counterfeit of virtue, which leads to the bondage of legalism.

When I served as dean of evangelism at Franciscan University of Steubenville, a sixty-seven-year-old priest showed up at the front door of my office. At the time I was doing a national radio program called "Purpose for Living." He had listened to me daily. and felt prompted to tell me, a young layman, of his problem with scrupulosity. I listened for an hour to the pain this man experienced. He was to blame for everything that was wrong around him. His every action seemed sinful. Even in the Sacrament of Reconciliation, he did not find freedom for his tortured soul.

I quickly saw that I did not have the ability to help this man, but I did have ears to listen. I hope I brought him some relief. I also was able to direct him to therapy and counsel from another priest. That man's scrupulosity is all too common among Christians.

Even an entire Christian group can suffer from the malady. Once my family and I visited such a group. At first it seemed filled with holy people, who quickly repented for wrongdoing, even in public. Their children seemed perfectly obedient.

Yet over time, we came to see these people were not free. They were behind prison bars—the bars of scrupulosity. They were repenting for the typical mistakes of daily life, not for objective sin that offended God and harmed the body of Christ. For instance, one child repented for complaining about the heat during school, while another repented for not sweeping the basement floor with diligence.

Like the people of the Galatian community, they had lost the freedom of the gospel. The words of St. Paul came to mind: "You foolish Galatians! Who has bewitched you? It was before your eyes that Jesus Christ was publicly exhibited as crucified! The only thing I want to learn from you is this: Did you receive the Spirit by doing works of the law, or by believing what you heard? Are you so foolish? Having started with the Spirit, are you now ending with the flesh?" (Gal 3:1-3).

What I saw in those people was not only bad piety, but bad psychology. Outside they looked perfect, but inside they were longing for love, affirmation, and freedom. They did not live by grace, which results from ownership and personalization, and heals the wound within.

We have examined together the critical need for taking responsibility in our own lives. We have seen the role that acknowledgment, ownership, and personalization play in living a healthy and fulfilled Christian life. We have also seen the danger of toxic shame and bad piety.

In my own life, I am continually trying to keep alive this understanding of personal responsibility. The older I get the more I comprehend the words of St. Paul and echo them with joy, "I am chief amongst sinners." But Paul's statement, now also mine, does not come out of self-denigration rooted in a poor self-image. Rather, it comes out of a realistic self-assessment. I can say it only because the love of God has set me free. He has given me his grace and power. This grace is manifested in my life most especially through a personal relationship with him. I meet him daily in prayer. I find him revealed in the glory of his creation. I find his very breath in his written Word.[8] I find his love revealed in other people and the ministry of his church.

Once I have acknowledged my personal responsibility, owned and personalized it, nothing has been as liberating for me as the Roman Catholic Church's ministry of the powerful Sacrament of Reconciliation. Through this sacrament, we can receive God's forgiveness for our sins, once we have confessed them to him and truly repented from the heart. That is good news! That is cause for joy! A taste of God's grace! That marvelous reality will be our next topic.

CHAPTER 7

The Forgiveness of Sin

Not only did G.K. Chesterton understand his sinfulness and desperate need for God, he also understood the marvelous reality of God's grace and mercy. Queried about his conversion to Catholic Christianity in middle age, his answer was as simple as it was profound, "... the forgiveness of sin."

Chesterton had developed a deep respect for what was then known as the Sacrament of Penance, now known as the Sacrament of Reconciliation. He had experienced the freedom and joy this sacrament brings when the penitent confesses his or her sins to the priest and receives God's forgiveness. Put another way, Christ had forgiven his sins through the sacramental agency of a priest, who represented the community of believers which is always injured by the sins of its members. Imagine the tremendous release of confession for the truly contrite sinner who has carried a heavy burden of guilt and sin! Imagine the renewed sense of oneness with God and one's brothers and sisters in Christ when that burden is lifted!

To Chesterton, and to me, hearing the words, "I absolve you, in the name of the Father, and the Son, and the Holy Spirit," had, and has, such a liberating effect. Oh, I know that it is God alone who forgives sin. I have heard the usual concerns of the

possible abuses of the confessional. And I am sure they sometimes occur. However, I need to hear with my ears, and not
just my heart, the profound truth of God's unconditional love.
God understood our need to see and believe, and therefore
came among us as a man (Jn 1:14). He carries on his ministry
through the body of his Son, using concrete signs and human
language, especially in the sacraments, to enflesh his presence
among us.

THE CORPORATE AND PERSONAL DIMENSIONS
OF FORGIVENESS

During Jesus' earthly ministry, many struggled with his
claim to forgive sins. The story of the paralytic is profoundly
instructive, for it demonstrates both the connection between
unforgiven sin and illness, and the nature and means of God's
forgiveness of sin.

A few days later, when Jesus again entered Capernaum, the
people heard that he had come home. So many gathered
that there was no room left, not even outside the door, and
he preached the word to them. Some men came, bringing
to him a paralytic, carried by four of them. Since they could
not get him to Jesus because of the crowd, they made an
opening in the roof above Jesus and, after digging through
it, lowered the mat the paralyzed man was lying on. When
Jesus saw their faith, he said to the paralytic, "Son, your sins
are forgiven." Now some teachers of the law were sitting
there, thinking to themselves,"Why does this fellow talk like
that? He's blaspheming! Who can forgive sins but God
alone?"
Immediately Jesus knew in his spirit that this is what they
were thinking in their hearts and he said to them, "Why are
you thinking these things? Which is easier: to say to the paralytic, 'Your sins are forgiven,' or to say, 'Get up, take your
mat and walk'? But that you may know that the Son of Man
has authority on earth to forgive sins...." He said to the para-

lytic, "I tell you, get up, take your mat and go home." He got up, took his mat and walked out in full view of them all. This amazed everyone and they praised God, saying, "We have never seen anything like this!" **Mk 2:1-12, NIV**

A number of important points about this encounter can teach us a lot about the nature of responsibility and forgiveness. First, the paralytic's friends brought him to the Master. Note that it wasn't easy getting him there. This point demonstrates that there is always a corporate dimension to our sin since it affects others. But there is a corporate dimension to our healing and forgiveness as well.

A great Christian hero of World War II, Dietrich Bonhoeffer, coined the phrase "cheap grace," which has deeply affected the way I view my faith. Bonhoeffer argued rightly that such a notion of grace was a contradiction of terms. And he was a man who suffered deeply for his own profession of faith in Jesus. Unwilling to cower when he saw millions of Jews being slaughtered, he put his life on the line and joined the resistance against Hitler. He understood grace. Yes, it is free. Yes, it is the unmerited favor of God. But it is by no means cheap. It was purchased by the precious blood of the Son of God. It is a priceless treasure. Bonhoeffer himself was executed only weeks before the Allied victory over the Nazis.

While forgiveness of sin and healing from the effects of sin do not come easily or cheaply, they are free to all who come to the source of grace, Jesus Christ. Those who join the faith community of the church are filled with the Holy Spirit and sent out to the nations to continue Christ's healing and saving work. As such we are called to be a healing community in a wounded world.

The apostles John and James tell us how important the healing community is in ministering the Lord's healing and forgiveness: "Is any one of you in trouble? He should pray. Is any one happy? Let him sing songs of praise. Is any one of you sick? He should call the elders of the church to pray over him and anoint him with oil in the name of the Lord. And the prayer offered in faith will make the sick person well; the Lord will raise him up. If he has sinned, he will be forgiven" (Jas 5:13-15, NIV). And again: "But if we walk in the light, as he is in the light, we have fellowship with one another, and the blood of Jesus, his Son, purifies us from all sin. If we claim to be without sin, we deceive ourselves and the truth is not in us. If we confess our sins, he is faithful and just and will forgive us our sins and purify us from all unrighteousness" (1 Jn 1:7-9, NIV).

Our second point is that there was a profound connection between the man's paralysis and his unresolved and unforgiven sin. Notice how Jesus first forgives the man's sin. Then physical healing follows. This can be the case in our own lives as well. Doubt, guilt, and toxic shame can have a devastating effect and block the healing God wants to give us. The way to complete freedom is through the one who himself told us, "... I am the way, and the truth, and the life" (Jn 14:6).

Medical science finally seems to be acknowledging the connection between emotional and spiritual well-being and physical health. The market has been flooded recently with books about this connection between mental, emotional, spiritual, and physical well-being. The entire "wellness" movement is based on an ancient Christian principle: we are not just a body—we are body, soul, and spirit. Every aspect of our person needs healing when we are sick. Jesus came to save the whole person, not simply to open the eyes of the blind and enable the lame to walk. The ultimate end of our life of faith is the resurrection of a glorified body and eternal life with God.

Jesus, God in the flesh, the one who was like us in all things, "yet without sin" (Heb 4:15) pronounced the words of freedom which the paralytic desperately needed to hear. Not only was he set free spiritually, he got up and walked! The miracle was controversial then. Should we be surprised that it still is today? "Now some teachers of the law were sitting there, thinking to themselves, 'Why does this fellow talk like that? He's blaspheming! Who can forgive sins but God alone?'" (Mk 2:6-7, NIV).

Jesus gave that same authority to those he would establish in authority in his body, the church, and those who would follow in succession to them. "Jesus said to them again, 'Peace be with you. As the Father has sent me, so I send you.' When he had said this, he breathed on them and said to them, 'Receive the Holy Spirit. If you forgive the sins of any, they are forgiven them; if you retain the sins of any, they are retained'" (Jn 20:21-23).

To my readers from traditions that don't recognize this sacrament, I am not trying to criticize your ecclesiology. But all Christian traditions can at least agree that forgiveness of sin through the redemptive act of Calvary is the source of true freedom. It provides freedom for the body, soul, and spirit.

A particularly effective use of the sacrament is a general confession, which should not be confused with the absolution of a group *without* individual confession to a priest. This ancient practice in the Catholic tradition provides an occasion when people can review their entire lives and confess any known sins privately to a priest. He, representing both Christ and the community of the faithful, listens with a compassionate ear and serves as a minister of forgiveness and healing. It is interesting to note that in the recovery community, this practice has been rediscovered. But often it is not used sacramentally among Catholics in recovery. Why? Because in many Christian circles, there appears to be a fear of integrating the Twelve-Step process and the Christian faith.

Step Five encourages us to "admit to God, to ourselves, and to *another human being* the exact nature of our wrongs"[1] (emphasis mine). In her wonderful treatment of Step Five in *Codependents' Guide to the Twelve Steps*, Melody Beattie shares her own experience of Step Five:

> Historically, religions have preached that confession is good for the soul. This is true. It is especially true for codependents, but let's reword it. Confession, honesty, and vulnerability are good for healing us and our souls.
>
> Some call codependency a disease, an illness. Others call it a problem. Some don't know what to call it. Some don't even like to call it "codependency." But many, including some original Al-Anon members call it a "soul sickness."

What we do in recovery is to practice the daily behaviors that we call "recovery." What we are seeking are psychic and soul level changes in ourselves, changes that can be manifested in our lives and our relationships, beginning with our primary relationships with ourselves.

If we have done the work called for in the Fourth Step, if we have sat down and inventoried ourselves, we have started to shake up our souls. We have reached in with a brillo pad and begun to scrub loose the debris and film within, those things blocking us from living the life we want. No matter what form of Fourth Step we use, no matter if we do a small, medium, or large one, we have loosened some things that need immediately to be washed away.

Once we start this process of loosening the "stuff" within, we will often notice it more. We may feel the weight of it all. We may begin to *notice* the feelings, needs, guilt, and burden of what we have carried around. We need to set up an appointment to talk about this soon. We need to move quickly onto this step to do the washing away and cleansing of all that has been loosened.[2]

What Beattie describes can be the experience of general confession. Yet this great treasure of the church has been left to gather dust. Perhaps that is one reason why believers are joining Twelve-Step programs in increasing numbers. The church has lost sight of the importance of her healing ministry in this and other ways.

MY EXPERIENCE OF FORGIVENESS

My family had all but abandoned practicing the faith when I was in the fifth grade, and we became what I call cultural Catholics.

After rediscovering my faith as a young man, I attended a large charismatic Catholic conference in Florida. There I heard Abbot David Gaerets, O.S.B., of the Benedictine monastery in Pecos, New Mexico[3] speak about the unconditional love of God and the forgiveness of sins. He opened my eyes to see not only the depth of my need for forgiveness, but the depth of my heavenly Father's love for me. At the end of his talk, he invited us all to take advantage of the sacrament.

Memories of my childhood rushed to my mind, both good and bad, as I got into line to go to confession. Born in 1954, I had experienced both the pre-Vatican II and post-Vatican II Roman Catholic Church. In my experience of both, there have been moments of great beauty and profound experiences of God, although Vatican II certainly ushered in a tidal wave of changes as well.[4]

I remember as a seven-year-old boy approaching the private confessional in the cold and dark sanctuary of St. Matthew's Church in Dorchester, Massachusetts. This was before Vatican II. I felt both fear and remorse—fear for having offended God by my sins, and remorseful contrition for my guilt. Fear and remorse—especially in a young, impressionable child—can easily cross the fine line between healthy and unhealthy shame.

Though already discussed in the last chapter, I believe that the importance of this distinction cannot be stressed enough. An example was recently brought home by an incident involving my two sons: Keith, who is eleven, and his brother Joel, who is three. They share a bunk bed—the scene of this particular crime.

Joel, who is every inch a little boy and the youngest of our five children, is rambunctious. Keith, whether he will admit it or not, goads him on. They regularly wrestle and, smaller and younger though Joel is, he holds his own—but not by following civilized standards of wrestling, which his older brother seems to believe he should know by osmosis. Instead, he attacks out of primal instinct—which is to say, with ferocity.

This particular day Joel jumped from the top bunk onto his brother's stomach, commando style. Keith quickly lost his temper and began repeatedly berating him: "Joel, *you're* bad... *you're* a bad boy!"

Laurine and I got the boys settled down, corrected and reconciled. Then we had a fruitful discussion with Keith. "Keith," I said, "we never told you when you were Joel's age, or have we ever, that you were a 'bad boy.' We told you when your behavior was bad. There's a big difference. Do you see the difference?"

Well, at first he didn't. But as we talked, he did. There is a difference—a big difference. It took me many years to discover it for myself. As a child I came to see myself as a bad boy and tried to compensate by being perfect. I was plagued by toxic shame. Though outwardly confident, I never really loved myself. I just couldn't measure up.

DRIVEN TO PERFORM AND OVERCOMING THE HURDLE MENTALITY

Even after I gave my life back to the Lord as a teenager, followed by years of inner healing and pastoral care, I retained a hole in my soul. My self-worth had improved somewhat, and I even had breakthroughs when I saw my worth in Christ. But subtly and slowly, I began to spiritualize my efforts at perfection and to admire my accomplishments as measures of my worth.[5] I tried to earn the affirmation of my peers and those who had authority over me. I became driven to perform perfectly.

Countless poor souls have taken the same frustrating, miserable path. It is doomed to failure; at least on this side of the tomb, none of us can be perfect in this way. Only the Lord performs perfectly. Certainly, he is bringing each of us to completion, and he is the one who will bring us through. We are works-in-process, clay in the Master's hands. The lie of the enemy from the beginning is that we could be perfect on our own (Gn 3).[6]

Neither can the world around us be perfect until it is created anew, once the sons and daughters of God—you and I—achieve completion and are revealed in glory. Hear this marvelous promise in the words of St. Paul:

> ... We are children of God, and if children, then heirs, heirs of God and joint heirs with Christ—if, in fact, we suffer with

him so that we may also be glorified with him. I consider that the sufferings of this present time are not worth comparing with the glory about to be revealed to us. For the creation waits with eager longing for the revealing of the children of God; for the creation was subjected to futility, not of its own will but by the will of the one who subjected it, in hope that the creation itself will be set free from its bondage to decay and will obtain the freedom of the glory of the children of God. We know that the whole creation has been groaning in labor pains until now; and not only the creation, but we ourselves, who have the first fruits of the Spirit, groan inwardly while we wait for adoption, the redemption of our bodies. For in hope we were saved. Now hope that is seen is not hope. For who hopes for what is seen? But if we hope for what we do not see, we wait for it with patience. **Rom 8:16-25**

Another obstacle to knowing the joy of God's forgiveness is what I call the "hurdle mentality," a variant on the main theme of perfectionism. When Laurine and I were first married, we spent much energy simply making ends meet. Within months our first child was on the way, and I was in my last year of college working full-time and taking twenty-one credit hours. She was on her feet as well—nine hours a day as a hairdresser.

We knew our pace of life was extreme, but we thought we had to endure it only for a while. We kept waiting for things to be normal. By normal we unknowingly meant perfect and ideal—an Ozzie-and-Harriet kind of home life.

Well, after college came law school. After our firstborn, Kristen, came our son Keith. "When we just finish law school," we thought, "then things will be 'normal.'" Then it was the bar exam—then our daughter, Ann—then my first important career job. As you can imagine, five children and sixteen years later, we are still not Ozzie and Harriet. But we are content and at peace.

Why? What changed? Not the world around us, but the world within us. First, we've stopped looking for the normal or ideal family life. We discovered along the way that we didn't know what the word normal meant, which is typical of adult children of dysfunctional families. So Laurine and I gave up our quest for the perfect life in this false sense. Oh, the drive still catches us every so often, but as long as we are honest with ourselves and God, we are able to steer our ship through troubled waters without capsizing.

For some time, we lived about forty miles from Pittsburgh, Pennsylvania, in Steubenville, Ohio. While there are some wonderful things about the Ohio Valley, especially its people, there's little culture. So as often as we could, we would head down Route 22 to Pittsburgh. First, we had to travel through Weirton, West Virginia, the only city in America where a major interstate ends in a two-lane road.[7] The road was filled with potholes, which resembled moon craters. Regular construction delays led to elaborate detours. My son, Keith, once decided the construction was a plot. They'd begin at one end of the highway and work all the way down and then start again, just to get us.

But you know, no matter how frustrating the drive, it always got us to Pittsburgh with its many fine restaurants, theaters, and other cultural attractions. And all our complaints about the potholes, detours, and the construction didn't make the ride any better. They simply robbed the trip of some of its joy.

The fact was, to get to Pittsburgh we simply had to go through Weirton, through the potholes, detours, and the road work.

Life is like that. It isn't perfect in this way, and is filled with hurdles. The wayfarers, you and I, are not perfect either in this false sense, although we are called to completion in God's sense. In a very real way, the journey not only teaches us to drive, it prepares us for our ultimate destination by teaching us how to handle the ride.

In his first letter to the persecuted and dispersed Christians of the early church, Peter explained the inevitability of suffering as well as its value:

Therefore, since Christ suffered in his body, arm yourselves also with the same attitude, because he who has suffered in his body is done with sin. As a result, he does not live the rest of his earthly life for evil human desires, but rather for the will of God.

Dear friends, do not be surprised at the painful trial you are suffering, as though something strange were happening to you. But rejoice that you participate in the sufferings of Christ, so that you may be overjoyed when his glory is revealed. If you are insulted because of the name of Christ, you are blessed, for the Spirit of glory and of God rests on you. If you suffer, it should not be as a murderer or thief or any other kind of criminal, or even as a meddler. However, if you suffer as a Christian, do not be ashamed, but praise God that you bear that name. For it is time for judgment to begin with the family of God; and if it begins with us, what will the outcome be for those who do not obey the gospel of God? And, "If it is hard for the righteous to be saved, what will become of the ungodly and the sinner?" So then, those who suffer according to God's will should commit themselves to their faithful Creator and continue to do good.

1 Pt 4:1-2; 1 Pt 4:12-19, NIV

Peter also explained the value of suffering and struggle in developing virtue and character:

His divine power has given us everything we need for life and godliness through our knowledge of him who called us by his own glory and goodness. Through these he has given us his very great and precious promises, so that through them you may participate in the divine nature and escape the corruption in the world caused by evil desires. For this very reason, make every effort to add to your faith goodness; and to goodness, knowledge; and to knowledge, self-control; and to self-control, perseverance; and to perseverance, godliness; and to godliness, brotherly kindness; and to brotherly kindness, love. For if you possess these qualities in increasing measure, they will keep you from being ineffective and unproductive in your knowledge of our Lord Jesus Christ. But if anyone does not have them, he is nearsighted and blind, and has forgotten that he has been cleansed from his past sins. Therefore, my brothers, be all the more eager to make your calling and election sure. For if you do these things, you will never fall, and you will receive a rich welcome into the eternal kingdom of our Lord and Savior Jesus Christ. **2 Pt 1:3-11, NIV**

We are in process and our life is indeed a journey. Rather than being clichés, these two truths are pivotal to our own sense of peace in life.

RECEIVING THE SACRAMENT OF GOD'S FORGIVENESS

A significant help in overcoming the drive to perform and the hurdle mentality is frequent reception of the Sacrament of Reconciliation. The sacrament can also aid one in overcoming toxic shame, low self-esteem, and scrupulosity. (These problems, however, may also benefit from long-term counseling.) The sacrament helps us take responsibility for sinful actions, and also provides the assurance of God's forgiveness. We can also come to see our own eternal value to the Lord, as well as our dignity and self worth.

I remember my brief experience of the then Sacrament of Penance as a fifth grader at Our Lady of Sorrows parish in Sharon, Massachusetts. My family had started to attend church infrequently. We children also began to attend public schools, and the influence of the church dwindled in our lives. Our parish had a young pastor, trained in pastoral practice and methodology based on the Second Vatican Council. My short experience of the sacrament under his ministry focused not only on my own culpability for sin, but its impact on the whole faith community—my family, friends, classmates, and neighbors. Perhaps even more importantly, it focused on the unconditional love of God and his readiness to forgive sin and heal its bad fruit. But that experience was too short-lived, had no lasting effect on me, and did little to undo my low self-esteem. Sadly, I carried that unwelcome baggage with me into adulthood.

Returning to my experience at the large charismatic Catholic conference in Florida, it had been ten long turbulent years since I had last gone to confession. Here I was, a nervous nineteen-year-old. I knew the ritual had changed. I remembered the old act of contrition taught to me by the Sisters of St. Joseph at St. Matthew's School: "O my God, I am heartily sorry for having offended You, and I detest all my sins, because of Your just punishments, but most of all because they offend You, my God, who are all good and deserving of all my love. I firmly resolve, with the help of Your grace, to sin no more and to avoid the near occasions of sin." Was it still all right to use that prayer? I wondered.

There were other changes to deal with. First, there was no confessional. I had heard an explanation of going to confession face to face, but I had never experienced it. During my years away from the sacrament, I had lived anything but a chaste life. As a teenage hippie, I had explored all the paths of understanding and enlightenment I could find in the Boston area. There were many, and they all led nowhere. I had traveled across the country, swept up in the counterculture of the day, and had found only emptiness. By God's grace, I had ended my journey at the foot of the cross of Jesus Christ—back home in the church. I was deeply sorry for the painful things that had happened along the way.

I had asked the Lord's forgiveness many times. Intellectually, and at a certain level in my heart, I knew that I had been forgiven, washed clean by the blood of the cross of Christ. But the experience of full freedom I had sought eluded me. "Maybe this time," I thought, "I'll really feel forgiven."

It was my turn! I walked into the cheery room, bright with filtered sunshine. A young priest, aware of my awkwardness, welcomed me in the name of Jesus and on behalf of the church. With trepidation I began in the words I remembered from my childhood: "... Bless me Father, for I have sinned, it has been over ten years since my last confession...."

The young priest smiled. "Tell me, what's your name?" he asked.

"Keith," I responded.

"Keith," he said, "do you know how much the Father loves you and how happy he is that you have come home?"

That was all I needed to hear. Tears welled up in my eyes and overflowed. I opened my heart. In a cathartic cleansing, I shared what I was holding deep inside and still feeling ashamed of. Staring downward, I opened my heart to this minister of Christ's love. It was as though chains that had been tightly wrapped around my heart burst apart. At the end of my litany of sin and failure, I looked up into the smiling face of that young priest and I saw his eyes. They looked strangely familiar to me. They looked like Jesus' eyes. For a moment, they were.

He spoke lovingly to me: "Are you genuinely sorry for your sin, Keith?" he asked me.

"Yes, I am, Father."

"And do you resolve with the help of God's grace to sin no more, and to avoid the occasion of sin?"

"Yes, I do."

"Then," he responded, "I absolve you in the name of the Father, the Son, and the Holy Spirit. You are free in Christ!"

All I can say is that joy unspeakable flooded my soul. He laid hands on my head and prayed for the power of the Holy Spirit to fill my life and give me strength to grow in holiness. Still smiling, he said, "Keith, as your penance, I want you to take a long walk this afternoon and simply rejoice in the Father's love for you and the beauty of his creation." I nearly floated out of the room after his warm embrace. I was filled with so much peace and joy. It was a new beginning.

Since that encounter with the compassionate, forgiving Christ, the sacrament has been a needed ally in my "struggle against sin" (Heb 12:4).

As I have been freed of a bad self-image and have begun to

overcome toxic shame, I have found the fear I once had of the sacrament has lessened. Frequent reception of this sacrament has been helpful in minimizing my predominant faults as well. My tendency toward compulsive overeating skirts dangerously close to the sin of gluttony. Discerning the difference between the two is not always easy. Confession gives me an opportunity to explore the differences between the two, with the counsel of a priest. Further, I am able to pinpoint occasions of sin and receive God's grace to avoid them in the future.

The sacrament is a tremendous weapon in my arsenal in curbing compulsive overeating and my other predominant faults, such as impatience and intolerance. I can't say that I have fully used it as such. Unhealthy shame still has a funny way of robbing me of God's best gifts. But I have seen what a treasure the forgiveness of sins truly is.

In receiving this great gift of forgiveness, I see that the Christian life must be one of continual conversion. It is about being born again and again and again. Noted theologian Alan Schreck explains it:

First, a Catholic can say "I have been saved." It is an objective fact that Jesus Christ already has died and been raised to save me from my sin. The salvation of the world has been accomplished by Jesus Christ. This salvation has already begun to take effect in the life of everyone who has accepted Jesus Christ and been baptized. As St. Paul said, "If anyone is in Christ, he is a new creation" (2 Cor 5:17). In this sense, I can say, "Yes, I have been saved."

Secondly, Catholics need to say that "I am being saved." We must realize that we are still "running the race" to our ultimate destiny of heaven. We must turn to the Lord each day for the grace to enter more deeply into his plan for our lives and to accept his gift of salvation more fully." And we all, with unveiled face, beholding the glory of the Lord, are being changed into his likeness from one degree of glory to another (2 Cor 3:18). In this sense, I can say, "I am being saved."

Thirdly, Catholics say that "I hope to be saved." We must persevere in our faith in God, love for God, and obedience to his will, until the end of our lives. We have hope and confidence that God will give us that grace, and that we will respond to it and accept his gift of salvation until the day we die. In this sense, "I hope to be saved."[8]

In 1979, John Paul II spoke to priests about the necessity of "being converted anew every day." He said, "If we have the duty of helping others to be converted, we have to do the same continuously in our own lives." He went on to give five meanings of conversion:

Being converted means returning to the very grace of our vocation. It means meditating upon the infinite goodness and love of Christ, who has addressed each of us and called us by name and has said, "Follow Me." Being converted means giving an account before the Lord of our hearts, about our service, stewards entrusted with the mysteries of God. Being converted means continually giving an account of our negligence, of our sins and our timidity, of our lack of faith, hope, of thinking only in a human way and not in a divine way. Being converted means for us seeking again the impartation and the strength of God in the Sacrament of Reconciliation and beginning anew. Being converted means to pray continually and never lose heart.[9]

Though my predominant faults are now very, very obvious to me, their impact is overshadowed by the wonderful realization of God's unconditional love and forgiveness. These faults act as thorns in my flesh, reminding me of my neediness—my continual need for conversion. One obvious thorn is my struggle with weight. Others are my impatience and intolerance. Let me share with you now some recent experiences with these flaws which illustrate an important principle in recovery and renewal: taking life one day at a time on our path toward recovery and renewal.

8

One Day at a Time

So do not worry about tomorrow, for tomorrow will bring worries of its own. Today's trouble is enough for today.

Mt 6:34

I WAS SEATED IN A SMALL OFFICE awaiting the arrival of a doctor I had never met. I had come with complaints of fatigue and a probable sinus infection. I've never liked physicals, and this one was particularly distressful because it was completely unexpected, plus I was new to the area. I had moved to the Virginia Beach area less than four months before, after being asked by Pat Robertson of the CBN network to head a new public interest law firm that would handle cases involving liberty, life, and family causes. We were caught up in finding schools for the kids, grocery stores, a church, and doctors.

The doctor rushed into the room, took his seat at a desk, and began to rifle through some paper work. I always expect the worst in doctor's offices. Would I find that my sinus pain was in fact a brain tumor? Was my thirty-seven-year-old heart acting more like a sixty-year-old one? After all, my father had just had a series of heart attacks, and he had never had physical problems before. Did I have a terminal illness like cancer? Such thoughts flashed through my mind like unwelcome billboards on a scenic country road.

The doctor poured through his notes and then delivered his findings: two sinus infections, a throat infection, and a polyp in the nasal passage. Why that took a full physical examination to diagnose I couldn't figure. I could have told him all of that.

He wrote out a prescription for a high dosage of antibiotics in characteristic doctor scrawl, which is both illegible and unaffordable.

DECLARED GUILTY OF "MORBID OBESITY"

The doctor wasn't about to stop there. Matter of factly, he spoke out loud as he wrote on my chart "morbid obesity." Well, I knew I was *fat*, but the phrase "morbid obesity" was both insulting and disturbing. All the way to the pharmacy to collect my antibiotics the words repeated themselves. Each time I felt more anger, sadness, disappointment, discouragement, and frustration.

Here I was sicker than a dog and desperately in need of rest, yet the most important thing in my life was that insulting medical assessment—"morbid obesity." But it captured the heart of my dilemma. I was fat again, trapped inside an overweight body.

Less than two years ago, I was, for me, a trim one hundred and eighty-five pounds on a six-foot frame. I was exercising daily and eating right. Now I had ballooned to two hundred and sixty-seven pounds. It was only one more time around on a merry-go-round I was tired of riding, but couldn't get off. I knew that this doctor's diagnosis had missed the mark. My weight was a symptom of a deeper malady. But knowing this was far from a cure.

I was a fat kid from a fat family. Yes, there is clearly a genetic link. But more significantly, as I had learned years earlier, there was a pattern of emotional and spiritual attachment, and a pattern of codependency. I would starve myself, consuming only liquids for months at a time. I had been on high protein diets, both the liquid and the solid kind. I would consume no carbohydrates and very little fat. I had prepared special diet shakes and abused my body by depriving it of basic nourishment. How many times I had said, after completing a weight-loss program, "Never again!" How many testimonies had I given of the success of this or that diet, of this or that new spiritual or psychological insight, of this or that recovery program? Yet here I was heavier than I had ever been.

My impulse was to try a quick fix. I would once again subject myself to the grueling regimen of a near-starvation diet and rigid exercise. I'd show 'em, I thought. Fortunately, I just as quickly asked myself, who are "they" and what did I have to show them? A sign of progress.

I reflected on my history of weight gain and weight loss. The last time I had lost a significant amount of weight I was hosting a national radio program called "Purpose for Living." And I was also practicing law, serving as a major administrator at the Franciscan University of Steubenville, serving as a lay leader in a large Christian group, and trying to love my wife and help raise our five children. I appeared to be the picture of success in the eyes of many. But this so-called success was not success at all.

In order to promote the radio program, I was committed to fundraising banquets in major cities. Its success was not dependent on the response of listeners, but upon the evaluation of its financial health by an administrator. Caught up in it all, I was working my heart out. My desire to share the gospel as a Catholic layman could finally be realized, I thought. The drivenness of the banquet scene, the consultants, and the fundraising made me uncomfortable, but I threw myself into it all. Slim and trim, I presented a marvelous appearance.

Unfortunately, my ego became as inflated as my frame had been. But God knew what I needed. He allowed difficulties and trials to cut my ego down to size, lest "after proclaiming to others I myself should be disqualified" (1 Cor 9:27). But now, my outward size had ballooned, even though my interior was in fairly good shape. What could I do?

Some readers may be thinking, "What is he saying? That God made him fat? Or that God made him fall? Either way that's heresy, isn't it?"

What I am saying is that because God is love, he is always doing the most loving thing. In that sense he does indeed turn "all things... together for good for those who love him" (Rom 8:28). In a very real sense, "Father knows best." Whatever it takes to make us like Jesus.

But just what is God's perfect will for me? It has not been laid out in an instruction manual. Rather, he has given me guideposts along the way, like the Scriptures, the teaching office of the church, my conscience, and the revelation of natural law. Some contemporary writers have helped to clarify this issue by discussing the permissive and providential will of God. In his providential will, God has a plan for each one of our lives, but it is up to us to cooperate with him. In his permissive will, he allows us to make choices and then abide by the consequences. He desires that our decision-making be transformed, so that the choices we make bring us closer to him and more in accordance with his plan. The marvelous thing is that God can make something truly beautiful out of our lives even when we make some wrong choices. The key is turning back to him.

For three years, God had been reminding me that weakness is the doorway to true strength. When we understand how desperately weak we really are without God, we are closer to him then we have ever been. That is the ultimate good. Augustine of Hippo wrote to his friend, Proba:

You may still want to ask why the Apostle [Paul] said: *We do not know what it is right to pray for*, because, surely, we cannot believe that either he or those to whom he wrote did not know the Lord's Prayer.

He showed that he himself shared this uncertainty. Did he know what it was right to pray for when he was given a thorn in the flesh, an angel of Satan to bruise him, so that he might not be puffed up by the greatness of what was revealed to him? Three times he asked the Lord to take it away from him, which showed that he did not know what he should ask for in prayer. At last, he heard the Lord's answer, explaining why the prayer of so great a man was not granted, and why it was not expedient for it to be granted: *My grace is sufficient for you, for power shines forth more perfectly in weakness.*

In the kind of affliction, then, which can bring either good or ill, we do not know what it is right to pray for; yet, because it is difficult, troublesome and against the grain for us, weak as we are, we do what every human would do, we pray that it may be taken away from us. We owe, however, at least this much in our duty to God: if he does not take it away, we must not imagine that we are being forgotten by him but, because of our loving endurance of evil, must await greater blessings in its place. In this way, *power shines forth more perfectly in weakness.* These words are written to prevent us from having too great an opinion of ourselves if our prayer is granted, when we are impatient in asking for something that it would be better not to receive; and to prevent us from being dejected, and distrustful of God's mercy toward us, if our prayer is not granted, when we ask for something that would bring us greater affliction, or completely ruin us through the corrupting influence of prosperity. In these cases we do not know what it is right to ask for in prayer.

Therefore, if something happens that we did not pray for, we must have no doubt at all that what God wants is more expedient than what we wanted ourselves. Our great Mediator gave us an example of this. After he had said: *Father, if it is possible, let this cup be taken away from me,* he immediately added, *Yet not what I will, but what you will, Father,* so transforming the human will that was his through his taking human nature. As a consequence, and rightly so, *through the obedience of one man the many are made righteous.*[1] emphasis mine

THE REAL ROOT OF MY PROBLEM: DEVOURING LOVE SANDWICHES

So what does this have to do with morbid obesity? Everything. Contrary to what many believe, being overweight may not indicate sloth or gluttony. I am a textbook example.

The working class family of my birth would not have been characterized as even middle class by many. As I've already mentioned, my father, an orphan at an early age, spent most of his childhood in a boarding school. "You had to grab the potatoes first" he'd say of his experience in the orphanage, "or there wouldn't be any left." No matter how strained the family budget became, Dad made sure there was always plenty of food on the table. But my family's preoccupation and even relationship with food was unhealthy. It became a substance to be abused.

As I shared earlier, my mother was the daughter of an active alcoholic. Her father spent his final years in our home and would come home drunk early in the morning. In addition, my father had a temper and exercised authoritarian control in the home, while my mother was an enabler and caretaker in an unhealthy way to both Grandpa and us kids. To top it all, we suffered through the trauma of watching our house burn and experienced seasons of financial insecurity. All of this made for a difficult and traumatic childhood.

I would realize consciously the profound effects only much later. The impact on my mother was also profound. She too is a compulsive overeater, along with my brothers and sisters. A codependent pattern.

We were always eating. We ate to celebrate, to relax, to mourn, to unwind, to fill the spiritual and emotional void, to soothe our depression and anger. Friends and neighbors said the Fourniers "knew how to eat." Nothing was farther from the truth. We ate compulsively. I didn't learn why until much later.

As a small boy, I ate mayonnaise sandwiches on cheap white bread. My father called them "love sandwiches." And so did I. The significance of the name became clearer when I recognized that food was a substitute for unmet needs in our lives. We ate spaghetti sandwiches as well, stuffing refined white-flour noodles between slices of white bread. The goal was to be full—no, "stuffed," as we would say. Yet the emotional and spiritual emptiness inside us remained unfilled.

My mother showed her love through feeding us. When we

moved to the suburbs, I had many friends from wealthy families who always wanted to eat at my house. Somehow they sensed the well-intended affection my mother showed in cooking and serving food. They happily chose spaghetti or potatoes with gravy over their own upper-class cuisine. As my mother would say, "We can always throw in another hotdog."

But it wasn't only the quantity of food which increased our weights, but the kind of food, and most importantly, our obsession with it. We had gravy ladled over every possible meat, including hamburger, and plenty of starchy foods like potatoes and noodles. When there wasn't enough meat, gravy would be smeared on white bread, with rave reviews from the kids.

When we weren't eating, our conversation regularly centered around food. Even while we were holding our stomachs in literal pain from having eaten too much, one of my parents or my older brother would comment about how good another meal would taste later on. We were no longer eating for nourishment in order to live, we were living to eat. I was never aware of how much eating preoccupied us until I left home. A recent visit from my parents brought back a lot of memories. Even after we all finished eating, my mom was telling us about her new kitchen appliance, the "Fry-Baby," which made preparing fried foods a cinch.

It was only in my thirties that I realized I had a "relationship" with a substance called food. My compulsive overeating has resurfaced again and again, even though I have followed the Lord most of my life. I need his help now more than ever to break this destructive cycle. I don't want to change out of guilt or self-hatred, but out of love for him and myself. I have begun to see a healthy way.

So I was morbidly obese! But not to worry, for "these momentary light afflictions produce within us an eternal weight of glory" (2 Cor 4:17). That morbid obesity was a thorn in my side, a healthy dose of reality. We all need someone who is greater than ourselves. As Thomas Aquinas said, "The Creator must be more perfect than anything he creates." I am sure the Lord God isn't morbidly obese, but his servant, Aquinas, was certainly known to be corpulent. And because I have been morbidly obese as well, I am always drawn back to the foot of the cross of his Son.

So it was back to aerobics, off the fat and carbohydrates, and back to my stack of recovery books. Back through the steps and the loving discipline of a good regimen. But no more "quick fixes," no more "white knuckles." His "power is made perfect in my weakness." It certainly would be nice if the weight came off and stayed off once and for all. But more importantly, this diagnosis of "morbid obesity" has brought me back to that paradoxical symbol of spiritual freedom, the cross. Once again I will cling to it, one day at a time.

LIVING ONE DAY AT A TIME

So weight is a barometer of sorts for me. Not of how close I am to God, but how I feel about myself. I sometimes have buried my sense of failure, fear, insecurity, and lack of confidence in pounds—pounds from compulsive overeating. Besides "quick fix" diets like the Stillman Diet, the Physician's Weight-Loss Diet, and the Scarsdale Diet, I have submitted my weight problem to pastoral care. Many in the name of helping have only compounded the problem by shaming me.

The worst experience of that was when I was told by a visiting lay leader that I should no longer teach in public because I had regained some weight I had lost on a fad diet. "After all," he said, "being overweight undermines your credibility." What hurt most about that encounter was not the toxic shame it engendered, but the impact on my view of God and my relationship to him. At the time, that lay leader represented God to me and he had no understanding of my weakness. I began to feel ashamed before the Lord. The passion of my life has been to share the good news. I am an evangelist to the bone! But I felt unworthy of God's service.

Of course, the scandal of this experience is obvious to me now. Of course, I am weak! If being perfect were either possible or a prerequisite to approaching or sharing about God, none of us would be able to fulfill the Great Commission. Thank God his power is made perfect in our weakness (2 Cor 12:9).

I have found, however, that the approach of this leader is not uncommon. Too many Christian circles are intolerant of weakness, wounds, and basic human frailty. As the popular saying goes, paraphrased here, we Christians tend to shoot our wounded. How unlike the Jesus of the Gospels this truly is. Consider the woman caught in the act of adultery. Did Jesus shame her, like the Jewish leaders who had humiliated her in public and clamored for her death? No, he forgave her and told her to go and sin no more.

One dangerous pastoral practice bears mentioning here. With the goal of helping people grow in maturity and character, leaders in some Christian groups have members make agreements about their weaknesses—for example, not to fall back into an area of sin or weakness. If the agreement is broken, it becomes a matter of wrongdoing—of sin and required repentance. As you can imagine, such an approach can lead to legalism and terrible bondage! It takes a weakness and makes it a sin! This practice can, if left unchecked, compound people's problems by engendering guilt, shame, low self-esteem, and even deceit in those who don't measure up.

Of course, gluttony is a sin. But my weight gain was not about gluttony. It was about codependency—about trying to fill a hole not in my stomach, but in my soul. But God is good! Even my continual struggle with weight can, and has, become a vehicle for his love. I know how much I need his grace one day at a time.

"One day at a time" is a motto in the recovery community, but it is much more than that. It is a lifeline in a Christian's walk with God. It's a hard lesson to learn.

In the late seventies Laurine and I received some very distressing news. Her parents were getting divorced. We tried everything we could to help. We prayed not only for their reconciliation, but for their conversion. We knew that it was going to take the miraculous healing of Jesus Christ to save their marriage, which had been on the rocks for years. Laurine's father had been an active alcoholic for years. That, along with many other unresolved difficulties, was bearing its ugly fruit.

As is often the case, the kids began to take sides and became part of the problem themselves. Laurine and I tried to avoid that danger by committing ourselves to loving them both no matter what. We decided to visit them to show our love.

We drove from our home in Steubenville to my mother-in-law's house in Peoria, Illinois. For weeks before, we had prayed not only to see them reconciled, but to see both of them discover God's love. We agreed Laurine's mother was more open to Jesus Christ. "After all," we reasoned, "Mom is the one who is least hardened of heart."

It was a painful time. We did everything we could to comfort Mom and bring joy and hope into her house. When the day came to meet my father-in-law, we were fearful of what to expect. Pat, Laurine's mother, had left the house, and her dad, Mac, was joining us for lunch.

We quickly saw that Mac was a broken man with a heart wide open. We shared a meal together and opened our hearts. We shared about our faith in Jesus Christ and his power to change anybody. We told him of the emptiness in our lives and how only God had been able to fill the holes inside.

Mac surprised us by being like a dry sponge, open to being filled with the waters of life. He shared his own pain, his dissatisfaction with his career, and his deep emptiness. He had spent so many years working for what? He didn't know what he was living for any longer. With the prompting of the Spirit, Laurine and I led Mac in a prayer of repentance and turning his heart to Jesus Christ as his Lord and Savior. God moved in a very powerful way. Tears flowed. We then shared with him how to nurture his rediscovered faith and follow the Lord one day at a time.

We told him how the Lord had miraculously provided for us in the early years of our marriage, day by day. That his grace was always present. To back up our statements, I opened the Gospel of St. Luke and read:

Then Jesus said to his disciples: "Therefore I tell you, do not worry about your life, what you will eat; or about your body, what you will wear. Life is more than food, and the body more than clothes. Consider the ravens: They do not sow or reap, they have no storeroom or barn; yet God feeds them. And how much more valuable you are than birds! Who of you by worrying can add a single hour to his life? Since you cannot do this very little thing, why do you worry about the rest?

Consider how the lilies grow. They do not labor or spin. Yet I tell you, not even Solomon in all his splendor was dressed like one of these. If that is how God clothes the grass of the field, which is here today, and tomorrow is thrown into the fire, how much more will he clothe you, O you of little faith! And do not set your heart on what you will eat or drink; do not worry about it. For the pagan world runs after all such things, and your Father knows that you need them. But seek his kingdom, and these things will be given to you as well.

Do not be afraid, little flock, for your Father has been pleased to give you the kingdom. Sell your possessions and give to the poor. Provide purses for yourselves that will not wear out, a treasure in heaven that will not be exhausted, where no thief comes near and no moth destroys. For where your treasure is, there your heart will be also. **Lk 12:22-34, NIV**

After hearing the passage, Mac stared at us incredulously. "Where is that?" he demanded. "It's right here in the Bible," I said.

"Is that a Protestant Bible?" he asked.

Laurine's Dad had been raised in a Protestant home that was deeply anti-Catholic. Before I met Laurine, she had given her life to the Lord at a Cursillo weekend. Cursillo is a movement within Catholic Christianity wherein people experience, over the course of a weekend, an evangelical encounter with Jesus Christ as their personal Lord and Savior. It had been a lifeline for my wife, who had been very successful as a hairdresser but was still empty and miserable inside. Though her father noted the change, he remained leery of her Catholic faith. When she met and married a Catholic, he grew to accept me, but not our church. Now that lifelong suspicion was impeding an evangelical moment.

"Show it to me in the Protestant Bible," he said.

"Sure, Mac, I'd be glad to," I said.

He brought down a dusty, old King James Bible from a shelf in the dining room.

I turned to Luke 12 and read the same words in the Old English translation.

"You're right," he said. "It's there."

"Yes, it's there, Mac," I said, "And so is the Lord. He's here, ready to guide you one day at a time."

We were able to get Mac an appointment with a local Methodist minister who headed up his church's "Road to Emmaus" program. He began his journey of faith. Though the divorce became final and the relationship is still strained, Mac has persevered over the years with the Lord. He sought help and is a recovering alcoholic. While his life has not been easy, Mac is no longer alone. The Lord is with him, one day at a time.

The Christian life is not about quick fixes, though they may occur. Miracles do happen, but most happen over time.

In a powerful Easter sermon preached by an early church bishop, Melito of Sardis, we hear about the Lord's triumph:

> The Lord, though he was God, became man. He suffered for the sake of those who suffer, he was bound for those in bonds, condemned for the guilty, buried for those who lie in the grave; but he rose from the dead, and cried aloud: Who will contend with me? Let him confront me. I have freed the condemned, brought the dead back to life, raised men from their graves. Who has anything to say against me? I, he said, am the Christ; I have destroyed death, triumphed over the enemy, trampled hell under foot, bound the strong one, and taken men up to the heights of heaven: I am the Christ.[2]

Christ is the one who can turn our struggles and sufferings into triumph. Sometimes the very things that we resent or fear become the vehicle for his revelation.

Prior to the conversion of St. Francis of Assisi, he hated lepers. Leprosy was feared because it was disfiguring and there was no cure. Contact with lepers was seen as sure death. It was the AIDS epidemic of Francis' time. Yet after Francis met the one who triumphed over death, his attitude was dramatically changed. In an encounter with a leper, though he was inclined to flee, the Spirit of God drew Francis to the man. Overcoming his repulsion and fear, he embraced the leper. When he opened his eyes, he saw the face of Christ in that leprous man.

We too can find Jesus in the face of those things which seem most difficult, just as my father-in-law did when he confronted a circumstance that seemed to present little hope. I shared with you about my family background that laid the foundation for my predominant fault of intolerance and impatience. I wish I could say that I have overcome my low threshold of frustration, but alas, I continue to struggle. Let me share with you a recent experience that shows the merits of facing this fault one day at a time.

OF LATE FLIGHTS, FOG, AND FRUSTRATION

I opened my eyes wide to read the luminous face of the alarm clock. It was three o'clock in the morning. Unable to fall back asleep because I knew the alarm was set for 4:15, I reluctantly got up. I knew it would be a long day. Hurriedly, I packed like an intruder in my own house, trying not to awaken my lovely companion in life and our five children. I snuck into the kids' bathroom to scrape my face with a steel blade, brush my teeth, and shower. I donned my court uniform—a two-piece, striped suit and polished black shoes. Then I crept downstairs to get a badly needed cup of coffee.

As quietly as the proverbial dormouse, I packed my garment

bag and large trial briefcase, left my traditional "I love you all" note on the kitchen table, and stole out into the early morning fog.

I knew that within a few hours the quiet of my home would be shattered by a steady, growing hum of activity. Kristen, our teenage daughter, would be primping herself for high school as though she were auditioning for Hollywood. Her sister, Ann, whose concern only yesterday was wrestling her older brother, would follow suit, complaining about the gaps in her teeth and the color and texture of her hair—but all with that silly and infectious grin which I hope she never loses. Number three daughter, MaryEllen, would just be waking up, her blond locks covering her cherubic eyes. The boys probably would be fighting. Keith would complain about having to wake up at all, and his three-year-old brother Joel would complain that Keith was being mean to him.

In the midst of the chaos would be Laurine who—after sixteen years of diapers, struggles, bills, pressures, and worries—looks more beautiful than the day I met her. She would be stuffing lunch bags, giving the kids directions, filling the cat's dish, and trying to maintain family peace and sanity in the mad dash for the school bus. It's a real and earthy picture, not unlike the incarnation when God manifested himself in the mundane.[3]

But I would miss all that today. As executive director of my public interest law firm, I had to be in Buffalo, New York, to help defend two Christian ministers who faced charges of civil contempt of court for allegedly defying a court order to prevent the blockade of an abortion clinic. In fact, they had not blocked the clinic but had passed out tracts in front of the clinic, exercising their first-amendment rights.

I had to be in court at nine. My first flight was to take me to Washington, D.C., and my second to Buffalo. I was armed with memoranda, legal cases, and a trial briefcase full of other legal ammunition. But things wouldn't go the way I thought this morning. As the French say so often, *"C'est la vie."* The older I get, the more I use those words. That's life, and it's full of surprises.

I knew when I pulled out of my driveway that the fog was unusually heavy, but it was only 4:30 and I had allowed plenty of time to negotiate Route 64 to the Norfolk, Virginia airport. After parking, I checked my luggage and went to my gate. Everything seemed in order, but at 6:15, an announcement came over the loudspeaker that my flight was canceled due to dense fog.

Hurriedly, I made my way to the counter emphasizing to everyone who would listen my need to get to court on time. The frustrated gate agent said curtly, "Sir, you aren't going to make it." It took me only a minute to vent an emotional outburst filled with anger, irritation, fear, depression, and just plain disgust. But to whom or what were my emotions directed? It certainly wasn't the gate agent's fault, or that of the airlines, or the pilot's. Fog is fog. It is neither good nor bad, it just is.

The gate agent, who was dealing with her own emotions, rerouted me through Baltimore. I rushed to the new gate only to find myself a participant in the game of "hurry up and then wait." After sitting on board through two delays, we were airborne. Proud that I had overcome an obstacle, I gloated as I read the morning paper.

Then the pilot interrupted my reading to announce that due to fog we would have to circle the city of Baltimore. After circling for an hour, we were sent back to Norfolk to wait in yet more lines.

At this point, I called my office to say that I was going home, but word from New York had come that the other lawyers voluntarily assisting the ministers still needed me. I boarded yet another plane, sat through two more delays, and finally landed at three in the afternoon—a full twelve hours from when I had first opened my eyes. Though frustrated and weary, I found myself reflecting over the day's events.

I thought back over the nineteen years since I renewed my decision to follow Christ. I thought of the seasons of spirituality

I had gone through. I thought of the various lenses I had worn through which I had viewed similar incidents in life. I recalled times like this when I knew for a fact I was being spiritually attacked. After all, I was about serving God, so his enemies were my enemies. I had cast down these enemies by taking authority in Jesus' name. I had quoted Scriptures and demanded my way like an adolescent discovering his or her autonomy. Well, I still believed in spiritual warfare. I still believed the devil opposes the things of God. But the presumptuousness and haughtiness which accompanied that earlier time had been softened through the mill of disappointment and the seasoning of experience.

Once I would have sought to discern what such thwarting meant, intensely searching my heart and the Bible for some deeper meaning and prophetic purpose. Perhaps I even would have called a spiritual leader and asked for his insights. Well, I still discern as I can. I still seek the prophetic in the circumstances of life. I still believe in spiritual leadership. But I have given up naiveté and stopped looking to human beings as gurus. Through the crucible of failure, I have learned to rethink adversity. Like the fog, it's part of the trip.

There was nothing very complicated about the fog. It was real, and it impeded free access to air travel on that particular day. What could I do about it? All my frustration and worry, in the words of the Master, "would not add a single cubit to my span of life."

Where was God in the midst of it? He was in my home in the eyes of my children who, like all children, reflect the continual freshness and wonder of the miracle of life. He was in the determined, committed service of their mother, whose love is incarnated in the daily sacrifice of herself for others, whether she feels like it or not—or whether she smiles or hollers while doing it. He was in the fog, revealing his omnipotence over the affairs of humans and their ingenious flying machines. And, last but not least, he was in my heart, seeking to have first place in my decisions, my reactions, my relationships, and my affection—seeking to bring the true peace which "passes all understanding."

Life is filled with late flights, fog, and frustration. It will be until the life to come. Yes, God can, and very often does, remove fog and protect our schedules. But, after all, he is God and can do as he pleases. I have learned that usually what must change is not the circumstances, but me.

That is the lesson to be learned from the fog, the flight, and my frustration. I need to trust, to persevere in work and charity, until I arrive. Then I need to love even more upon arrival. It is a lesson that can't be learned if every day is clear, if every flight is on time, and life is free of frustration.

Socrates believed that children are born with all the knowledge in the universe, but as their lives progress, they forget. The role of the teacher is to call it back to mind. His pedagogical approach still survives, particularly in law school. I will never forget the shock of my first semester in law school. After undergraduate work, where the norm was a professor giving a lecture while the students took notes, I wasn't prepared for the socratic dialogue between professors and students. We had hundreds of pages of reading nightly in an almost undecipherable and technical language, with the expectation that by the next day we not only had read all the cases, but were able to draw out the issues and key legal principles in classroom discussion. Halfway through the first semester, it began to click, almost as if my brain shifted. I began to understand the language and discern the guiding principles.

Sort of like life isn't it? With time, complex things become simpler than you expected, and others more complex! Take parenting, for example, especially when the kids enter their teenage years. Yet you chart a course through the fog and frustration, guided by the light of his love.

We can chart our course only one day at a time. We continually will be tempted by the tyranny of tomorrow. However, faith compels us to pick up our cross daily and follow after him whose "yoke is easy and burden is light" (Mt 11:30).

To accomplish this shift in perspective, we need a fresh new way of thinking. (See what the apostle Paul says about this in Romans 12:2-7.) We need to begin seeing things from a heavenly perspective—from the perspective of faith. For me, this has sometimes been like putting on new glasses—the title of our next subject.

Putting on New Glasses—Seeing Anew with the Eyes of Faith

We walk by faith, not by sight. **2 Cor 5:7**

I T WAS A GRAY, OVERCAST Saturday morning in late March. I had just been to my weekly counseling session. As I shared earlier, this counseling came at a critical time in my life. My world had collapsed. I had experienced failure at work, in my personal life, in my family life, and in lay ministry.

My counselor had helped me understand that this time of collapse was actually a gift from God. It enabled me to finally see codependent patterns in my life. I had been so successful in many different endeavors, in spite of codependency, that I hadn't yet seen clearly its destructive effects on my life.

Having experienced a breakthrough that morning in understanding how codependency operated in my life, my mind was racing at one hundred miles per hour, even though I was driving down the highway at the speed limit, on my way home. My thoughts were on fast-forward and I couldn't stop the tape. All the pieces of the puzzle that made up my life were finally beginning to fit. I had an exhilarating sense of spiritual freedom and release.

Traveling down Route 7, leaving East Liverpool and heading

toward Steubenville, I began to thank the Lord out loud for the insight I had just received. Grace fell like water on my parched desert. I had been in such emotional pain for months that I was even doubting God's love for me.

Overwhelmed by the experience, I decided to stop for a cup of coffee. Up ahead to my left I noticed "Buddie's Hamburgers," a little restaurant on the outskirts of East Liverpool. The parking lot was deserted. Assuming I would find the privacy I wanted, I pulled in, parked the car, and entered. At the counter, I ordered a large cup of black coffee and grabbed the last copy of the local paper from the dispenser, looking forward to a time of solitary reflection when I could savor my insights.

Cup in hand, I made my way over to the farthest table in the place and opened the paper. I did not really focus on the articles, but let my breakthrough experience trigger a flood of memories.

My solitude was short-lived. Shattering my reverie, were these words, "You almost done with the paper?" Startled, I looked up. Far across the room was a frail, white-haired woman, whose looks belied her loud, piercing voice. She shouted again, "Are you almost through with that paper, son?"

I muttered a few words like, "Well,... yes...." She made her way across the dining room and sat directly across from me in the booth.

"I'm stuck here," she said. "Ernie blew up my car engine and it's in the shop."

Especially at this personal moment, I was, for one of the few times in my life, at a loss for words. "I am sorry to hear that, Ma'am," I said haltingly.

"That's OK," she replied. "You see, he drives my car a lot. Ernie is seventy-nine years old. The other day he was driving down 7 here through East Liverpool and the red oil light went on in the car. He just kept driving all the way through Steubenville and all the way on to Mingo Junction. You know what that old codger did? He blew the engine."

I didn't know how to respond to her presence or her comments, but I sensed that she wouldn't leave, and I was right.

"You know," she went on. "I told that Ernie he needed his eyes checked. Well, I was right. You know what? The next day he went to the eye doctor, and he got himself fitted for a new pair of glasses. Well, after wrecking my car, he told me he didn't even see the red light on the dashboard. But now, he says, *his whole world looks different.* Since he got new glasses, he says, his whole world looks different."

Still startled, I tried to respond. "Well," I said, "I hope you get your car fixed and here's the newspaper."

"Thanks a lot, son," she said.

I sat and drank my coffee, but rather than risk further encounters, I decided to leave for home. I bid farewell to my newfound friend on the way.

"Thanks for the paper," she said.

"No problem," I responded. "Can I give you a ride?"

"No, Ernie's coming to get me," she said. "And now that he has those new glasses I know he's going to arrive."

I walked through the parking lot, chuckling at what had just occurred. "What a nice old woman," I mused. As I drove out of the lot and back onto Route 7, I started to think about my bottoming out over the last year.

I was beginning to understand the compulsive patterns in my life, how they had developed, and how I could begin to overcome them. I was beginning to see the effects of my childhood on patterns of codependency that had developed in adulthood. I was beginning to see the truth about, yes, my weakness, but also my strengths and how they could be maximized.

My life, which for so long had appeared to me as a half-empty glass, was beginning to look half full instead. I was actually happy again. I was starting to feel good about who I was and who I could be. I could look back now not with the pain of regret, but with the appreciation that can come only from a new perspective—a perspective of faith.

ADJUSTING OUR PERSPECTIVE

Then it hit me. "Since he got new glasses, his whole world looks different." That's it, I thought! I got new glasses and my whole world looks different. Since that experience, I have seen the importance of continually examining how I look at things and adjusting my perspective as needed.

I have since wondered whether that sweet old lady was, in fact, an angel. The author of the letter to the Hebrews reminds us: "Let mutual love continue. Do not neglect to show hospitality to strangers, for by doing that some have entertained angels without knowing it" (Heb 13:1-2).

This lady certainly fit the bill. Through her simple comments, God showed me a profound insight. I had needed new glasses. I had needed a radical change of perspective. God had given me new glasses. Things were beginning to look different in my life. I was starting to see his handiwork in the midst of my difficulties.

Have you seen those little cryptic signs that at first glance look like a series of vertical and horizontal bars, but as you look closer, you can make out the name Jesus? They're common these days in Christian offices. Even now when I see those little signs, at first glance I don't see the name "Jesus" until I look closely at the pattern. There's a great lesson in those little signs. Whether we recognize his presence or not, if we are Christians, Jesus Christ dwells in our midst. He is with us in our struggles, but to see him we need new glasses.

In chapter nineteen of the First Book of Kings, Elijah flees to Horeb in dire straits. So difficult is his predicament, we read, Elijah "was afraid; he got up and fled for his life" (1 Kgs 19:3a). And later:

He came to a broom tree, sat down under it and prayed that he might die. "I have had enough, Lord," he said. "Take my life; I am no better than my ancestors." Then he lay down under the tree and fell asleep.

All at once an angel touched him and said, "Get up and eat." He looked around, and there by his head was a cake of bread baked over hot coals, and a jar of water. He ate and drank and then lay down again.

The angel of the Lord came back a second time and touched him and said, "Get up and eat, for the journey is too much for you." So he got up and ate and drank. Strengthened by that food, he traveled forty days and forty nights until he reached Horeb, the mountain of God. There he went into a cave and spent the night.   1 Kgs 19:4b-9, NIV

In a mighty display of God's power on Mount Carmel, Elijah had exposed the idol Baal and his prophets as fakes. In so doing, he had confronted Ahab, the apostate king of Israel, with his sin and had enflamed the wrath of Queen Jezebel, the wicked and powerful woman behind the throne who now sought Elijah's life.

Elijah was holed up now in a cave. While he huddled in that darkness, the Lord appeared to Elijah and asked him what he was doing. As he shared his heart and his fears, the Lord directed him: "Go out and stand on the mountain before the Lord, for the Lord is about to pass by" (1 Kgs 19:11).

Elijah obeyed and left the cave. He made a conscious decision to find God in the midst of his struggle and fear. He stood on the mountain and listened intently for God's word. Still he did not find the direction he sought.

Then a great and powerful wind tore the mountains apart and shattered the rocks before the Lord, but the Lord was not in the wind. After the wind there was an earthquake, but the Lord was not in the earthquake. After the earthquake came a fire, but the Lord was not in the fire. *And after the fire came a gentle whisper.* When Elijah heard it, he pulled his cloak over his face and went out and stood at the mouth of the cave. Then a voice said to him, "What are you doing here, Elijah?"   1 Kgs 19:11-13, NIV, emphasis mine

The Lord finally gave the direction Elijah sought. That direction spared his life, and brought it new meaning. The Lord literally gave Elijah a travel map. He showed him how to avoid the wrath of Jezebel and gave him a companion to assist him in his prophetic ministry, Elisha. In the midst of the most difficult situation in his life, God came through for Elijah. So it is with us. We need to persevere through the darkness, climb the mountain, and then listen for God's direction.

But notice where Elijah found the Lord's direction. It came not in the wind, a mighty earthquake, or a mysterious fire, but in a gentle whisper. Very often the direction we seek for our lives will not come through some dramatic event, but in everyday happenings, the whispers we can easily miss.

Regarding faith, in *Evangelical Catholics,* I wrote:

For modern minds, *heart* is often reduced to a technical interpretation. When we hear the word, we frequently think of the physical organ and its blood-pumping function. At times we may even think of it in relationship to our emotions. But most of us rarely think of the theological truth that *heart* also represents the deepest reality or core of who we are as people. Paul understood this, however, and so must we. When we talk about believing in Jesus "in our hearts" and allowing Him to be "Lord of our lives," we are really inviting Him to rule over our entire beings, even to its very depths. This complete surrender begins in our hearts through *faith*; then, like the rippling effect caused by a stone tossed in a lake, it affects every facet of our being, our personality, and our behavior. This kind of surrender is essential to understanding evangelical Christianity fully. And it's the key to the proper integration of the Christian interior life and social activity. It's in this sense that Mother Teresa "believes in her heart."[1]

What an amazing perspective God has given to Mother Teresa of Calcutta, who listens for the whisper of God in the most dire of circumstances. An article in my morning paper of May 11, 1992, reads: "Nuns at Mother Teresa's mission sifted through heaps of wet clothes Sunday after a fire destroyed two roomfuls of donated garments. 'By the grace of God not much damage was done as the firemen came immediately and brought the fire under control,' said Mother Teresa, whose missionaries of charity run homes for insane women, hospitals, and orphanages." In the midst of adversity, Mother Teresa always seems to find triumph and a perspective guided by faith in God and his purposes.

Many years ago I was visiting my dear friend, Chuck Colson. A man who stood at the pinnacle of power as an advisor to then President Richard Nixon, Colson found himself in jail after being implicated in the Watergate scandal. Stripped of everything, he met Jesus Christ in prison and is now a prolific author and founder of an international ministry called Prison Fellowship.

The first thing I noticed about Chuck's office was a carved wooden sign on his desk which read, "Faithfulness, not Success." Once I asked him, "Chuck, where did you get the sign?" It gave him the opportunity to share with me a wonderful story about Mother Teresa.

On an American tour in the early 1980s, Mother Teresa was asked by a reporter, "To what do you attribute your success?" To which Mother Teresa responded, "What success? I don't see the word success in the Bible, only faithfulness. It's faithfulness, not success, that I'm committed to." So taken with those words was Chuck Colson that he had the phrase carved into a block of wood to keep before him while at work.

Inspired by Colson's example, I decided to have a plaque made with those same words for my desk. It reminds me that in a world driven by a desire to succeed, we who follow in the footsteps of the greatest success of all history, Jesus Christ, need to be faithful in the midst of failure, struggle, pain, and darkness.

St. Paul reminded the Corinthian Christians:

Consider your own call, brothers and sisters: not many of you were wise by human standards, not many were powerful, not many were of noble birth. But God chose what is foolish in the world to shame the wise; God chose what is weak in the world to shame the strong; God chose what is low and despised in the world, things that are not, to reduce to nothing things that are, so that no one might boast in the presence of God. He is the source of your life in Christ Jesus, who became for us wisdom from God, and righteousness and sanctification and redemption, in order that, as it is written; "Let the one who boasts, boast in the Lord." 1 Cor 1:26-31

Christian faith is a puzzle to those whose eyes have not been opened to the victory of the cross. In the same letter, Paul reminded the Corinthians and all of us:

For since, in the wisdom of God, the world did not know God through wisdom, God decided through the foolishness of our proclamation, to save those who believe. For Jews demand signs and Greeks desire wisdom, but we proclaim Christ crucified, a stumbling block to Jews and foolishness to Gentiles, but to those who are the called, both Jews and Greeks, Christ the power of God and the wisdom of God. For God's foolishness is wiser than human wisdom, and God's weakness is stronger than human strength. 1 Cor 1:21-25

The truth of this message must take root deep inside our hearts and grow into a tree whose branches stretch through every fiber of our being. Then we will always know God's presence in the midst of our lives. Through the eyes of faith, we will know who is really in control.

DEVELOPING A FAITH PERSPECTIVE

Of the biblical definitions of faith, the one that helps me most is in the letter to the Hebrews, "Faith is being sure of what we hope for and certain of what we do not see" (11:1, NIV). Faith is evidence or proof that God is at work in our lives. For the believer, then, faith in God supplants the need to see, hear, or touch God. Eventually, we no longer need tangible evidence because faith itself becomes the evidence. We walk by faith, the Scripture tells us, and not by sight.

After the disciple Thomas has touched the wounds of the risen Christ, the Lord Jesus asks him: "Have you believed because you have seen me? Blessed are those who have not seen and yet have come to believe" (Jn 20:29).

As a young man, I heard a Baptist pastor tell a story which illustrates that kind of faith. Two old men were traveling up a mountain in the midst of a terrible rain storm. The rain and the winds made their climb extremely difficult. Fatigued and discouraged, half way up the mountain, one turned to the other and said, "This is a very steep mountain, and I am not sure that I can make it to the top." His friend responded affectionately, "If you have trouble, I'm by your side." A short time later, the ferocity of the wind and the rain increased to the point where the men were literally being blown about. Again, the same man turned to his friend and said, "This is terrible wind and rain, I don't know if we can make it to the top." And again his friend responded, "What wind? What rain? I grew up in weather like this. We'll make it."

The story drives home a very important point. Our perspective is often fashioned by our background and life experience. The friend understood wind, rain, and struggle. "He grew up in weather like this." In our lives, we need to come to understand and accept struggle based on a conscious decision that God, our friend, will help us work in and through rough weather. Our task is not just to find him in the midst of it, but to lean on his shoulder as we climb the mountain. This requires not only a change in our worldview, but the development of what I call a "faith view."[2]

I know that I did not "grow up in weather like this." I did not learn to find meaning and purpose in suffering until I began to see it demonstrated in the lives of others. Consider my friend Fr. Philip. He had developed a faith view that enabled him to experience God's presence even when he was in extreme pain, though he had every good reason to complain. Our lives are filled with men and women who have testified to this reality.

One is a hero of mine, Dr. Martin Luther King, Jr., who declared:

> A positive religious faith does not offer an illusion that we shall be exempt from pain and suffering, nor does it imbue us with the idea that life is a drama of unalloyed comfort and untroubled ease. Rather, it instills us with the inner equilibrium needed to face strains, burdens, and fears that inevitably come, and assures us that the universe is trustworthy and that God is concerned....
>
> Religion endows us with the conviction that we are not alone in this vast, uncertain universe. Beneath and above the shifting sands of time, the uncertainties that darken our days, and the vicissitudes that cloud our night is a wise and loving God. This universe is not a tragic expression of meaningless chaos but a marvelous display of an orderly cosmos....[3]

This is God's perspective on tragedy and difficulty in this life. If we hold onto this faith view, we can weather the storms of life, as have the great Christian men and women who have gone before us.

Using the life of St. Paul and the early Christians as examples, Dr. King said:

> Our capacity to deal creatively with shattered dreams is ultimately determined by our faith in God. Genuine faith imbues us with the conviction that beyond time is a divine Spirit and beyond life is Life....
>
> The Christian faith makes it possible for us nobly to accept that which cannot be changed, to meet disappointments and sorrow with an inner poise, and to absorb the

most intense pain without abandoning our sense of hope, for we know, as Paul testified, in life or in death, in Spain or in Rome, "that all things work together for good to them that love God, to them who are the called according to his purpose."[4]

The lives of many Christian heroes have appeared to be failures. They have not succeeded in the world's eyes. Yet those who persevered have found in this life the "peace that passes understanding" and in the life to come an eternal reward. That's key to this new perspective, to a faith view. One has to believe in eternity—in heaven.

In his essay, "The Weight of Glory," C.S. Lewis—one of the great Christian apologists and thinkers of modern times—expounds on the vision of glory that awaits us and how that ought to inform our lives, especially our relationships with others:

It is a serious thing to live in a society of possible gods and goddesses, to remember that the dullest and most uninteresting person you can talk to may one day be a creature which, if you saw it now, you would be strongly tempted to worship, or else a horror and a corruption such as you now meet, if at all, only in a nightmare. All day long we are, in some degree, helping each other to one or other of these destinations. It is in the light of these overwhelming possibilities, it is with the awe and the circumspection proper to them, that we should conduct all our dealings with one another, all friendships, all loves, all play, all politics. There are no *ordinary* people. You have never talked to a mere mortal. Nations, cultures, arts, civilisations—these are mortal, and their life is to ours as the life of a gnat. But it is immortals whom we joke with, work with, marry, snub, and exploit— immortal horrors or everlasting splendours. This does not mean that we are to be perpetually solemn. We must play. But our merriment must be of that kind (and it is, in fact, the merriest kind) which exists between people who have, from the outset, taken each other seriously—no flippancy, no superiority, no presumption. And our charity must be a real and costly love, with deep feeling for the sins in spite of which we love the sinner—no mere tolerance, or indulgence which parodies love as flippancy parodies merriment. Next to the Blessed Sacrament itself, your neighbour is the holiest object presented to your senses. If he is your Christian neighbour, he is holy in almost the same way, for in him also Christ *vere latitat*—the glorifier and the glorified, Glory Himself, is truly hidden.[5]

We see the infinite value and worth of each human being expressed in the parable of the lost sheep (Lk 15:1-7). Jesus tells us that God is like a shepherd who goes in search of one lost sheep and leaves the other ninety-nine. Thus the Good Shepherd shows the depths of his personal and tireless love when one of us strays from him. He shows us that he is not simply a mighty God of law and majesty who rules over the universe, but the lover of each of our souls. The Pharisees, who thought themselves to be righteous, didn't understand the reality of God's personal love and muttered, "This fellow welcomes sinners and eats with them" (Lk 15:2b). They did not have God's mind on the intrinsic value and worth of sinful human beings whom God had sent his only Son to save.

The parable of the lost coin deals with the same principle. We see the importance of pursuing those who have not found the way into the fold and of giving up all else until the lost one is found.

In the beautiful parable of the prodigal son, Jesus gives us an even fuller understanding of the heart of God. We meet the older brother, the perfect one of the family. He is embittered that his profligate brother is returning home and being welcomed back into the family without question. So caught up is he with his own righteousness that he cannot show the compassion demonstrated by his father. The lost son could be any one of us. It took pain, humiliation, and struggle to put him in a position of powerlessness, repentance, and humility—the position that unlocks that door to God's freedom and acceptance.

The loving father, who spares no expense in celebrating the lost son's return, of course, is God the Father who loves each of us unconditionally.

These characters present us with a new perspective of faith —a new way of viewing what is needed to transform our lives: surrendering our own agenda, embracing faith in a loving God, and being honest about our own condition.

I can certainly identify with the lost son. Prior to my teenage conversion I wandered aimlessly throughout the country. My eating day-old bread on a beach in Santa Cruz, California, is not that dissimilar to the prodigal eating corn husks with the pigs. I realized that my own efforts at finding the promised land had come up empty and returned to the faith of my childhood and to the Lord who is the center of it all.

Like the older brother, many years later, after having tried to follow the Lord faithfully, I had become blinded by pride and my accomplishments. I had become self-righteous, convinced that I had earned my position. I had become a Pharisee.

I have seen the love of the father in the parable in men like Fr. Philip Bebie who loved me unconditionally. In the embrace of that love, I have experienced the power and freedom of God the Father's love for me. *I have come to know that real power comes from my powerlessness when I receive God's love unconditionally.*

REAL POWER COMES FROM POWERLESSNESS

A joy I had for several years was serving on the editorial board of *New Covenant* magazine, a popular magazine serving the Catholic charismatic renewal. A column by its editor, Jim Manney, demonstrated marvelous insight regarding the source of real power in Christ:

We think we're in charge. We spend our days trying to change things. But can we? How much of our lives do we really control? Isn't the idea that we have power over people and circumstances basically a delusion, a fantasy of mastery that we cannot make real? This is the essence of the recognition of powerlessness.

The Bible and Christian tradition don't present heroic individual action as a religious virtue. Wise and righteous men and women submit to God's authority. Christ came to serve, not be served. To an exceptionally difficult divine call, Mary gave the perfect response: "Be it done unto me according to thy will."

But our faith also teaches us that powerlessness is the key that unlocks power—real power. Powerlessness is a paradox.

Christ's submission broke Satan's power. Mary's acceptance ushered in the Savior of the world. Abraham's obedience caused a people to be born. Moses' compliance set the captives free.

And so it is with us. The notion that *we* are in charge may be a fantasy, but the understanding that all things unfold according to *God's* plan raised the possibility that what we do might have some real effect. If followed out, powerlessness teaches that in weakness is strength. It also teaches that our efforts to change—conformed to God's will, directed as God would direct them—will be fruitful.

The second of the Twelve Steps says: "We came to believe that a power greater than ourselves could restore us to sanity." When we know we are powerless, we're able to know where real power lies.

Some say that the Twelve Steps of Alcoholics Anonymous, especially the first, will be the one enduring contribution of the twentieth century to the development of spirituality. If so, it will essentially be ancient wisdom stated in words that a power-obsessed age understands.[6]

I am convinced that we blame God for the wrong things. God is not at fault for the suffering and struggle of the human race—the human race is. There is a law at work in our midst which resulted from the rebellion of our first parents. That law or seed of rebellion thus became the tragic inheritance of all human beings. The apostle Paul anguishes over this internal struggle between good and evil in his letter to the Romans.

> I do not understand my own actions. For I do not do what I want, but I do the very thing I hate.... I can will what is right, but I cannot do it. For I do not do the good I want, but the evil I do not want is what I do.... So I find it to be a law that when I want to do what is good, evil lies close at hand. For I delight in the law of God in my inmost self, but I see in my members another law at war with the law of my mind.... Wretched man that I am! Who will rescue me from this body of death? Thanks be to God through Jesus Christ our Lord!
>
> ... There is therefore now no condemnation for those who are in Christ Jesus. For the law of the spirit of life in Christ Jesus has set you free from the law of sin and of death. ... To set the mind on the flesh is death, but to set the mind on the Spirit is life and peace. **Rom 7:15-25; 8:1-2, 6**

This "law of sin and death" affects each one of us, and, in fact, all of creation:

> For the creation was subjected to futility, not of its own will but by the will of the one who subjected it, in hope that the creation itself will be set free from its bondage to decay and will obtain the freedom of the glory of the children of God. We know that the whole creation has been groaning in labor pains until now; and not only the creation, but we ourselves, who have the first fruits of the Spirit, groan inwardly while we wait for adoption, the redemption of our bodies. For in hope we were saved. Now hope that is seen is not hope. For who hopes for what is seen? But if we hope for what we do not see, we wait for it with patience. **Rom 8:20-25**

As a father, husband, and manager, daily life presents plenty of opportunities for my buttons to be pushed. Intolerance, harshness, and impatience seem to crouch at my door. The desire to eat compulsively rears its ugly head when I'm under pressure at work and at home. The law of sin and death is very much at work within me still. I need the eyes of faith and the help of God to master my weaknesses. I need to cry out to the Lord in my powerlessness.

True spirituality, true faith, is the way to deal with the bad fruit of this "law of sin and death." It is the way through the pain and struggle of our daily life, with our wrong decisions, and compulsive behavior patterns. True faith recognizes that real power comes from powerlessness.

As Jim Manney said, "It is a series of daily, sometimes hourly decisions, to 'let go and let God.'" It is the path to genuine serenity and peace. It proclaims that in every circumstance, no matter how painful, God is there.

Corrie Ten Boom had this faith view. In one of her books, *The Hiding Place*, she described her painful stay in a Nazi prisoner-of-war camp with her sister, Betsie. There Corrie, though physically healthy, experienced a deep travail of soul. Betsie—who was wasting away from a protracted illness in an appallingly inhumane environment—comforted her sister. "There is no pit too deep, that God isn't deeper still," she replied to Corrie's questioning.

Betsie's words answer the perennial question, "Where is God in the midst of our pain?" He is right in the center of it, bearing it with us, transforming it when we unite it with the pain suffered by his Son on our behalf.

A FAITH VIEW IS ULTIMATELY AN ETERNAL PERSPECTIVE

Let's revisit the marvelous story of Lazarus, found in the eleventh chapter of St. John's Gospel. I believe this account is one of the most powerful in all four Gospels. It provides insight into how we can develop this faith view, an eternal perspective.

Picture the scene. When Lazarus, a friend of Jesus, was dying, his sisters, Mary and Martha, sent word to Jesus that he was sick. "But when Jesus heard it, he said, 'This illness does not lead to death; rather it is for God's glory, so that the Son of

God may be glorified through it.' Accordingly, though Jesus loved Martha and her sister and Lazarus, after having heard that Lazarus was ill, he stayed *two days longer* in the place where he was" (Jn 11:4-6, emphasis mine).

Think of it. How would you have viewed the Lord's behavior? He stayed there for two more days! Yet the Word of God tells us that he loved Martha, Mary, and Lazarus. When he finally decided to return to Judea, he told his disciples, "Our friend Lazarus has fallen asleep but I am going there to awaken him" (Jn 11:11).

Jesus knew that Lazarus was dead. Once again, the disciples did not understand. Yet it is interesting to note the response of Thomas, often referred to as "Doubting Thomas." When Jesus announced that he intended to go back to Judea, a place of danger where they could all lose their lives, Thomas said, "Let us go also, that we may die with him" (Jn 11:16). Perhaps Thomas' doubting had a much deeper purpose in his life, as it can in each of ours. Doubt, rather than being an enemy to faith can become one of its greatest allies. It's a question of how we respond to it. Do we give in to despair, or do we relentlessly pursue the truth and eventually own and personalize our faith?

When Jesus arrived at Lazarus' home, his friend had been dead for four days. Martha, in anguish, cried out,

> "Lord, if you had been here, my brother would not have died. But even now I know that God will give you whatever you ask of him." Jesus said to her, "Your brother will rise again." Martha said to him, "I know that he will rise again in the resurrection on the last day." Jesus said to her, "I am the resurrection and the life. Those who believe in me, even though they die, will live, and everyone who lives and believes in me will never die. Do you believe this?" "Yes Lord...." **Jn 11:21-26**

When he arrived at the tomb, we read two of the most powerful words recorded in all of sacred Scripture: "Jesus wept."

The human Jesus wept for the loss of Martha and Mary and the loss of his beloved friend. And the divine Jesus wept, and weeps, because he shares the pain of those he loves. Even the unbelievers realized, "See how he loved him." But then they went on to mock him saying, "Could not he who opened the eyes of the blind man have kept this man from dying?"

Finally, we see God's power and mercy demonstrated by Jesus:

> Jesus, once more deeply moved, came to the tomb.... "Take away the stone," he said.... "Did I not tell you that if you believed, you would see the glory of God?... Father, I thank you that you have heard me. I knew that you always hear me, but I said this for the benefit of the people standing here, that they may believe that you sent me.... Lazarus, come out!" The dead man came out, his hands and feet wrapped with strips of linen, and a cloth around his face. Jesus said to them, "Take off the grave clothes and let him go."
>
> **Jn 11:38-44, NIV**

This is true love! This is true power! This is the way through death's door! Not only the death that comes with our last breath, but the daily dying that comes with our being mortal. We must believe in the ultimate triumph of God's love. Jesus in his humanity and divinity had the faith view of the death that faces each of us. He is our perfect example.

Though we do not understand many things that happen in our lives, they can provide the opportunity for the glory of God to be revealed, if we choose daily, hourly, minute by minute, to let God in.

In chapter nine of the Gospel according to St. John, we read about a man who was born blind. A challenge to our faith is trying to understand how an innocent human life, from the womb, can be so afflicted. The reactions of Job's friends to his tribulations illustrate the many ways people have attempted to explain unmerited suffering (see Job 4-30). Their answers have always fallen short. So it was certainly understandable that the disciples of Jesus asked him, "Rabbi, who sinned, this man or his parents, that he was born blind?" (Jn 9:1).

Jesus responds: "Neither this man nor his parents sinned; he was born blind so that God's works might be revealed in him" (Jn 9:3).

Jesus then restored the man's sight and led him to conversion, revealing himself to the man as the Messiah. He gave him new glasses, both physically and spiritually. For every individual who experienced physical healing during Jesus' ministry, or who still experiences this kind of miracle, there are countless others whose spiritual sight has also been restored. Restoration of this kind of sight is miraculous as well. I am one of those individuals.

I can now look back on that season of failure and collapse in my life as a blessing. Believe me, when I was in the midst of it, it seemed like anything but a blessing. However, now I see the good fruit that has been borne in my life and in my family's life. I wouldn't trade it for the world. God has a plan for each of our lives which we can see, if we but view problems with the eyes of faith.

God in his mercy and love continues to restore sight to the spiritually blind. He awaits our request. He calls us to acknowledge both our position and his position—our powerlessness and his power.

Jesus asked his disciples a question he asks every one of us today, "Who do you say I am?" (Mt 16:13). The disciples gave various replies, so do we. Some said that he was a great prophet, but it was the answer of Simon Peter that Jesus was waiting for: "You are the Messiah, the Son of the living God."

You can almost feel the joy in the heart of God incarnate as he responded: "Blessed are you, Simon, son of Jonah! For flesh and blood has not revealed this to you, but my Father in heaven. And I tell you, you are Peter, and on this rock I will build my church, and the gates of Hades will not prevail against it. I will give you the keys of the kingdom of heaven and whatever you bind on earth will be bound in heaven, and whatever you loose on earth will be loosed in heaven" (Mt 16:17-19).

This encounter is so rich with meaning. But here we want to focus on how Peter is a model for us all in our walk of faith. He did not leave that encounter and live a perfect life, but struggled to the very end, as we have already seen. But what had become different about Peter? His faith. Jesus had given him new glasses. He had an eternal perspective. He began to see in his own life the fulfillment of the Lord's Prayer, "Thy Kingdom come, thy will be done, on earth as it is in heaven."

We, like Peter, have a perspective that will determine how we face challenges. Is our glass half-empty or half-full? Is our pain useless or useful? Is our God really in control? Each one of us longs for a faith perspective. Our hearts feel hope when we see it in the lives of others. But faith ultimately is a gift, not of our own making, but something that we take from the outstretched hand of our heavenly Father. "So faith comes from what is heard, and what is heard comes through the word of Christ" (Rom 10:17). We can say yes or no to that message, but faith itself is a divine gift. In that sense, we are ultimately powerless to make it happen.

When we respond to God's unmerited grace, we hear Christ's Word in Scripture, in the teaching of the church, in the inner sanctuary of our conscience, in our heart where his Spirit dwells, and even in our struggles.

For the man or woman of faith, death is not an end, but a beginning. Suffering, struggle, and pain are not mistakes, but signposts along the road that leads to eternity. But if you are like me, you discover down that road that you are inclined toward unhealthy ways of living.

The source of these propensities may not be objective sin, but an enemy called codependency in the recovery community. Let me share with you why sin and codependency are like kissing cousins and can easily be confused. Knowing one from the other can mean the difference between lasting healing and freedom or a continuing sense of frustration and failure—all because we don't understand our root problem and how to address it.

Codependency and Sin—Kissing Cousins

For I have the desire to do what is good, but I cannot carry it out. For what I do is not the good I want to do; the evil I do not want to do—this I keep on doing.

Rom 7:18b-19, NIV

I T WAS EASTER MORNING, and I was nine years old. I rubbed the sleep out of my eyes. I had not had slept much, filled as I was with the excitement and anticipation of a morning that was always special in my home. No matter how strapped we were financially, Easter and Christmas brought lavish expressions of love. The deprivation my father experienced in boarding school made him determined that his children would experience abundance at least twice a year. Also I believe that knowingly or unknowingly, Dad knew in his heart that he was to demonstrate the generous love God the Father had, and has, for each of us.

In the wee hours of the morning, we kids would steal our way downstairs to see what treasures awaited us. In what appeared to us a vast living room, we would find huge baskets filled with candy. Not that we kids needed sweets, since each of us struggled with a weight problem, but in another sense, we did need it. It was a demonstration of love.

THE HOLLOW BUNNY SYNDROME

This Easter morning the spread looked particularly bountiful. I rushed over to the basket marked "Keith." I gleefully examined the contents. In the middle of my basket, I found a large chocolate bunny. The first question that popped into my little head was, "Is it a solid bunny this year?" You never knew. Solid or hollow, those chocolate bunnies always looked the same. The only way to find out was to bite into it, so I bit my chocolate bunny's head off. You can imagine my disappointment when I discovered it was hollow inside.

That bunny has become a symbol for me. Just as you can never tell from a chocolate Easter bunny's exterior whether it's solid or hollow, I have come to see that many times I have been a hollow bunny. On the outside I looked very solid and substantial, but inside I was empty. And how deep that emptiness went! It was a gnawing hole.

A similar emptiness is inside each of us. Blaise Pascal called it a "God-shaped vacuum." To fill it, we resort to all kinds of distractions. But God alone can fill the void.

St. Augustine, in his well-known prayer, declared, "Our hearts are restless O God, until they rest in thee." Just as it is in physics that nature abhors a vacuum, our human hearts and souls abhor a vacuum. We were made for God. He and he alone is our destiny. He and he alone can satisfy the hunger in our hearts. Anything else we use to fill that vacuum rivals God for his rightful place at the center of our lives.

A book that deeply affected my teenage journey toward faith was *The Seven Storey Mountain*, by Thomas Merton. It details his amazing journey from a worldly intellectual to a Trappist monk who burned with love of God. I remember Merton's impression as he first set his eyes upon a sign over the door of the Gethsemane Abbey, a Trappist monastery in Kentucky. It read,

"God alone." That motto became the passion of Thomas Merton's life. I have often thought since then that it should be the passion of every Christian's life. Indeed, of every human being's life. Yet substitutes for God abound. One is only pretending to fill the hole when using material that will not satisfy.

I experienced a tremendous filling as a teenager when I returned to the foot of the cross and the heart of the church. I began to give God room in the center of my life, but I discovered that giving him room there is a daily choice, and many forces compete for a place in that inner sanctuary.

THE OBSTACLES OF SIN AND TEMPTATION

Our Dilemma. Many years back noted psychologist Karl Menninger wrote a book entitled *Whatever Became of Sin?* What became most valuable to me was the title of the book itself as a comment on society. Dr. Menninger asked a question that many people are now asking. Even within the contemporary Christian church, you find very little mention of sin. Yet if we do not understand the reality and impact of it, we cannot fight against it. Further, if we do not understand the distinction between sin and temptation, we can get very confused.

Finally, with a growing understanding of codependency, the picture can become even more confusing. You see, codependency and sin are often so intertwined, they are indeed kissing cousins.

One of the television programs I enjoyed as a boy is still in reruns. It's *The Patty Duke Show*. Patty and Kathy are cousins who look so strikingly similar, they easily get mistaken for each other. That's what it is like with codependency and sin. If we do not understand which is operating in a particular situation, we can get confused and fail miserably since we have not attacked the root problem. Let's first consider sin.

In many ways and for a variety of reasons we have violated God's laws ever since our first parents, Adam and Eve, defied God in the garden of Eden (Gn 3). Our inheritance is a mixed

one: though created in God's image, we suffer from a cor-
rupted condition that separates us from our Creator and
makes it easy for us to rebel against him. Not only has this condition created a chasm between us and the Lord, but it has sep-
arated us from ourselves, from our friends, from our spouses,
from our neighbors, and from our world. Now instead of a natural tendency toward transparency and intimacy, we hide our
true selves and tend to play the games of blame, denial, and
control. *Death,* which means "separation" in Scripture, has become a painful reality. "Just as sin came into the world through
one man, and death came through sin,... so death spread to all
because all have sinned" (Rom 5:12).

While humans are dead in sin and need new life (Eph 2:1-6;
Col 2:13), this does not mean that we are unable to respond to
God. The key is finding a way to be reunited with God.

Another biblical view confirms this. We are sick with sin and
in need of healing (Mk 2:17). We are impoverished by sin and
need God's riches (Lk 4:18; 2 Cor 8:9; Eph 2:7). We are pol-
luted or defiled by sin and need to be cleansed (Mk 7:14-23;
Eph 5:25-27; Ti 1:15; 1 Jn 1:7-9). We are lost in the darkness of
sin and desperately need the light of Christ (Jn 8:12; 12:35).
We are blinded by sin and need our sight restored (Lk 4:18; 2
Cor 4:3-6). We are enslaved to sin and need to be liberated
from it (Lk 4:18; Jn 8:31-36, Rom 6:16-18).

Because every aspect of the human person has been affected by sin, we need to be sanctified or purified entirely. Our
mind, emotions, will, body, and soul have all been affected by
sin, but sin has not destroyed our inherent goodness and the
abilities God has given us.

In short, we have dug ourselves into a pit so deep we can't
climb out of it. But because we are God's children and his
image bearers, we are not *totally* depraved.

God's Solution to Our Dilemma. How can we get out of the pit
of sin? We need a Savior to pull us out. But this person can't be
someone who shares the pit with us. This deliverer must be
above the pit, without stain of sin. He also must be able to
bridge the chasm between God and humanity, between holi-

ness and corruption. We need a God-Man, a sinless Savior. Jesus Christ fits this description, having revealed his identity in word and deed as the Son of God incarnate. When we freely place our trust in him, we are lifted out of the pit. As St. Paul tells us, "By grace you have been saved by faith, and this is not your own doing; it is the gift of God" (Eph 2:8).

The fact is we all struggle with sin. But God can use this struggle in our lives if we submit to his discipline:

> In your struggle against sin, you have not yet resisted to the point of shedding your blood. And you have forgotten that word of encouragement that addresses you as sons: "My son, do not make light of the Lord's discipline and do not lose heart when he rebukes you, because the Lord disciplines those he loves and he punishes everyone he accepts as a son." Endure hardship as discipline; God is treating you as sons. For what son is not disciplined by his father? If you are not disciplined (and everyone undergoes discipline), then you are illegitimate children and not true sons. Moreover, we have all had human fathers who disciplined us and we respected them for it. How much more should we submit to the Father of our spirits and live! Our fathers disciplined us for a little while as they thought best; but God disciplines us for our good, that we may share in his holiness. No discipline seems pleasant at the time, but painful. Later on, however, it produces a harvest of righteousness and peace for those who have been trained by it.
>
> Therefore, strengthen your feeble arms and weak knees. Make level paths for your feet, so that the lame many not be disabled, but rather healed. **Heb 12:4-13, NIV**

The good news is God our Father can use even our struggle with sin to refashion us into the image of his divine Son Jesus. This involves discipline, but it is rooted in our heavenly Father's unconditional love, which is not that of a shaming, dysfunctional parent. Instead, it is a love we can entirely count on since God has our best interests in view.

Temptation. But temptation and sin are not the same. All of us are tempted. A lustful thought or a malicious, yet juicy piece of gossip enters our minds. Do we reject it, or do we entertain it? It becomes sin when we cross the line and entertain it. The choice is ours. Jesus himself experienced many temptations, yet he did *not* sin. The author of the letter to the Hebrews in the New Testament tells us: "Because he himself suffered when he was tempted, he is able to help those who are being tempted" (Heb 2:18, NIV). Later on he states: "For we do not have a high priest (Jesus) who is unable to sympathize with our weaknesses, but we have one who has been tempted in every way, just as we are—yet without sin. Let us then approach the throne of grace with confidence, so that we may receive mercy and find grace to help us in our time of need" (Heb 4:15-16, NIV). Jesus understands. He's been there.

The fundamental issue is how we handle temptation. Temptation affects our decision-making. If it is at work in our lives and we are not fully aware of it, it can be a powerful persuader, prodding us to make wrong choices and even helping us to pursue destructive lifestyles. The key is recognizing when we are tempted to sin and nipping it in the bud. At the moment of temptation, we need to turn to Jesus our Savior and cry out to him for grace and mercy.

But first we have to acknowledge that sin is real. In a wonderful discussion on freedom from sin, the Catholic theologian Alan Schreck tells us:

Why can't we love God, others, and ourselves as we would like? Sin is the reason. Sin not only injures and disfigures us but it offends God, our good, all-loving Father. The horror and stupidity of sin is that instead of accepting God's love and favor, we turn our backs on him and cut ourselves off from the source of life and mercy. Sin is like slapping Jesus in the face, or driving the nails further into his pierced hands. Christians must detest sin, realizing what it really is and what it does to us.[1]

In the old "Act of Contrition," which Catholics used to pray during the Sacrament of Reconciliation, we read, "O my God I am heartily sorry for having offended you, and I *detest all my sins...*"(emphasis mine). We must grow to detest sin and make every effort to avoid occasions of temptation. When, by grace, we begin to overcome temptation and sin, we are on the road to conversion and renewal. That is what it means to "fight the good fight of the faith" (1 Tm 6:12).

However, another enemy has insidiously robbed me of the freedom that is mine as a son of God. This enemy sometimes looks like sin, can easily be mistaken for the flesh, and even masquerades as the devil. What is this enemy? Codependency, the "kissing cousin" of sin.

CODEPENDENCY AND ITS BAG OF TRICKS

Codependency is slippery and difficult to define. I am reminded of the Supreme Court Justice who in attempting to define pornography is reported to have said, "It is hard to define, but I know it when I see it." Codependency originally referred to those who were secondarily affected by someone else's primary addiction. For example, the spouse of an alcoholic, or the spouse of one who was chemically addicted, was viewed as codependent. It was obvious that the spouse—and, in fact, the whole family—was deeply affected by the addiction, not just the addict. However, as an understanding of families as systems began to develop in the 1960s, a fuller understanding emerged.

For example, my grandfather's active alcoholism affected the entire family. The way my parents responded to it directly affected the way us kids were raised. For one thing, the "no talk" rule was instituted as our usual approach to burying and denying problems like my grandfather's alcoholism. That has now carried over into my life, creating problems in the next generation.

The addiction itself caused a reaction in those who were

immediately affected by it and became the symptom of a bigger problem. This is what John Bradshaw calls "the disease behind the disease." The family system was not healthy and that lack of health affected everyone in the family—children and adults alike.

Perhaps one of the more interesting treatments of this problem is detailed by Charles Parker, the author of *Deep Recovery*. In a newspaper interview carried by *The Virginian Pilot*, on April 8, 1992, he called for getting rid of the "baggage of terminology." He said, "Take codependency—please. There is no such thing as codependent. You are just dependent. If your partner is addicted to something, you are not codependent on the alcohol... you are dependent on your partner. And take 'dysfunctional' too. I look at it not as 96 percent of us are living in a dysfunctional family, but that 100 percent of us are seeking balance in our lives. We are all recovering from something."

Dr. Parker continued, "What we don't realize is that it is not the 'thing' we are addicted to. It's the relationship." Dr. Parker's thinking is similar to that of John Bradshaw, a pioneer in the recovery movement. Bradshaw, speaking of his own alcoholism, admits to having been in recovery for years before he discovered, "the disease behind the disease," codependency.

Granted, we are called to be dependent, in the right way, upon God, recognizing our powerlessness and giving over to him our misguided efforts at control. Codependency, however, is an unhealthy dependency which gives rise to an unhealthy relationship or series of relationships. I myself had to recognize, for instance, that I had an unhealthy relationship with food, and so did the other members of my family of origin.

I believe that authors Drs. Robert Hemfelt, Frank Minirth, and Paul Meier, defined the term best in their landmark book, *Love Is a Choice: Recovery for Codependent Relationships*. Codependency is an "addiction to people, behaviors or things... the fallacy of trying to control interior feelings by controlling people, things and events on the outside."[2]

This definition contains a key to unlocking one of the

biggest problems in dealing with struggle and pain. We also see one of the greatest obstacles to filling the hole in our soul. The first time I read Drs. Hemfelt, Minirth, and Meier's definition of codependency, I knew they were speaking of me. I couldn't remember not feeling a deep emptiness inside—the hollow bunny syndrome. I had tried to fill that emptiness with many things. Some were well intended, many were destructive. In my wish to be candid about suffering, struggle, recovery, and renewal, I have shared many of them with you. Today I know that my compulsive overeating and flirtations with substance abuse were symptoms of codependency, as were other compulsions and my drive toward perfect performance.

I finally realized that I couldn't change the world, but I could change myself, if I responded to the grace of God. That is, I partially realized it as a teenager, which returned me to faith in Jesus Christ. After that conversion, I thought I had filled the hole in my soul, only to discover my soul had a leak. Slowly, over the years of trying to follow the Lord, I started to run on empty again.

There was one constant external indicator that something was wrong. At every point in my life where I began to face internal struggles that had become unmanageable, I would fall back into a codependent relationship with food.

However, I did not fully understand what was going on. I treated my overeating as a sin and felt increasingly guilty about it all. But I was only hurting myself. I was being driven by a pattern of codependency and not the sin of gluttony and sloth. I had picked up an old shoe from my family of origin, and I kept putting it on. The problem was not what I was eating, but what was eating me. No matter how I tried to handle it, real progress eluded me. Each time after I went on a fad diet, I gained the weight back. Besides the obvious physiological damage, damage to my self-esteem was enormous.

I became a hollow bunny. I had covered my emptiness with layers of chocolate. I appeared to be a Christian whose life was in order, except for being overweight at times, but I had fallen into the trap of legalism—or mere external compliance with God's laws.

Legalism leads to self-righteousness, the greatest impediment to holiness. It was the disease that infected the lives of the Pharisees. But for our purposes here, this legalism or external compliance was dangerous because it masks our real problems and prevents our facing them, as in my own life.

Melody Beattie, one of the most insightful writers on codependency, describes it well:

> Many good definitions of codependency have surfaced. In 1987, a handout at a week-long training seminar on chemical dependency and the family, sponsored by the Johnson Institute of Minneapolis, described codependency as "a set of maladaptive, compulsive behaviors learned by family members to survive in a family experiencing great emotional pain and stress.... Behaviors... passed on from generation to generation whether alcoholism is present or not."
>
> Ernie Larsen, the recovery pioneer from Minnesota, calls codependency "those self-defeating learned behaviors or character defects that result in a diminished capacity to initiate, or participate in, loving relationships."
>
> A friend, and recovering woman, defines codependents as "people who don't take care of themselves, whether or not they are, or have ever been, in a relationship with an alcoholic."
>
> And in *Codependent No More* I called a codependent "a person who has let someone else's behavior affect him or her and is obsessed with controlling other people's behavior."[3]

All these definitions are helpful in giving us a fuller understanding of codependency and how it operates. We can begin to see a way out of our predicament. Rather than trying to control ourselves, other people, and our own compulsive habit patterns, we can learn what it truly means to be powerless and surrender to God. Instead of being victimized by circumstances and others, we empower ourselves and begin to set new boundaries. We learn to say no to the excessive demands of others.

We rid ourselves of denial, avoidance, and control and learn once again to express how we truly feel. We discover who we really are and learn to love ourselves and accept God's unconditional love for us. We stop punishing ourselves through a false sense of guilt and toxic shame. We begin to realize how, like temptation, codependency can be an enabler, prodding us toward wrongful behavior. We stop expecting perfection, in the false sense of the word, from ourselves and others. We grow in tolerance and healthy expectations of ourselves and others.

I am reminded of a saying attributed to John XXIII, the source of which I have never been able to find. "See everything, overlook a great deal, and change a little." There is a lot of wisdom in this saying; it is like the Serenity Prayer: "God grant me the serenity to accept the things I cannot change, the courage to change the things I can, and the wisdom to know the difference."

I have begun to experience true freedom from codependency as I've grown to understand the difference between sin and codependency. Tragically, many people today are as confused as I was about these kissing cousins. They struggle with compulsive and destructive patterns in their own lives and attempt to resolve them as matters of sin, calling for confession and repentance of every compulsive act. What they really need to do is acknowledge their powerlessness over their addiction or compulsion, and then seek real understanding and help from God and those who are recovering from the same compulsion or addiction. That may well mean joining a Twelve-Step group. It may also call for long-term individual counseling. Yet some even slip into another dangerous spiritual disease that I've mentioned, scrupulosity—blaming themselves all the time for everything. That's craziness!

Melody Beattie comments further about what happens when we start recovering from codependency:

> We stop reacting to the powerfully dysfunctional systems so many of us have been affected by. We stop getting tangled up in craziness. We acquire the art of removing ourselves as victims.

We stop compulsively taking care of other people and we take care of ourselves. We learn to be good to ourselves, to have fun, and to enjoy life. We learn to feel good about what we've accomplished. We stop focusing on what's wrong and we notice what's right. We learn to function in relationships. We learn to love ourselves, so we can better love others.

Recovery also means addressing any other issues or compulsive behaviors that have cropped up along the way. Codependency is sneaky and deceptive. It's also progressive. One thing leads to another, and often things get worse.

We may become workaholics, or busy freaks. We may develop eating disorders or abuse mood-altering chemicals. We may develop compulsive sexual behaviors or become compulsive about spending, religion, achievement, or appearance.

Other complications can emerge too. We can become chronically depressed, develop emotional or mental problems, or stress-related illnesses.

"We hear a lot about how alcoholism is terminal for the alcoholic," says one recovering man. "We don't hear enough about how codependency can be terminal too. So many of us wind up thinking about, or trying to, kill ourselves."

Recovery means dealing with the entire package of self-defeating, compulsive behaviors, and any other problems that may have emerged. But we don't deal with these behaviors or problems by thinking we're bad for having them. We address ourselves, and recovery, with a sense of forgiveness and a certain gentleness toward ourselves. We begin to understand that the behaviors we've used were survival tools. We've been coping. We've been doing the best we could. We've been protecting ourselves. Some recovery professionals suggest these behaviors may have saved our lives.

"If we hadn't protected ourselves, we may have given up or developed a fatal illness and died," says Bedford Combs.

Whether it's a compulsion to caretake, control, work, or eat pecan pies, compulsive behaviors initially are about stopping the pain. We begin to realize what we've been doing: trying to stop the pain. But we begin to understand something else too. Although compulsive behaviors may help us temporarily avoid feelings or problems, they don't really stop the pain. They create more. They may even take on a habitual and problematic life of their own.

In recovery... we learn we are responsible for our behaviors, and our behaviors have consequences. We learn some behaviors have self-defeating consequences, while others have beneficial consequences. We learn we have choices.

We also learn we don't change by ourselves, or by exerting greater amounts of willpower. Intertwined with this process of changing our behaviors is a Higher Power, God, as we each understand Him. Paradoxically, we change most during those tremendous moments when we *run out of will-power.*[4] **emphasis mine**

Let me share with you, one of those times when I ran out of willpower. It was a time when my whole world seemed to fall apart, but which today I see was a great gift from God. It has taken the new glasses we spoke of in the last chapter to see that with force and clarity. Today I can finally say that the pain of that time was a price well worth paying, given the result.

THE INTERVENTION

Remember my telling you about that cold March day when two well-intentioned friends confronted me with what they regarded as a problem with alcoholism? Because of what I have learned, I know that they were quite simply, wrong. They were trying to rescue me without any real understanding of what was wrong with me.

Yes, I was in a downhill spiral. But why? Because I had "run out of willpower." I had steadily built a veneer of external compliance to the Christian life. Out of willpower I had attempted to conquer many things in life and accomplish great things for God. But those great things turned out to be failures—or so it seemed to me at that time.

In every area of my life, I had hit rock bottom, even in my family life. Yet I had shared month after month on the EWTN network about the family as the domestic church.

As my oldest child entered her teenage years, I began to discover how little I really knew about raising teenagers. I remembered words of wisdom from Dr. Jim Dobson, a dear friend and the founder of Focus on the Family—a well-known ministry to Christian families. In his office, he told me about his crucial decision to stop traveling at one point in his ministry. If he did not slow down and spend more time with his family, he would become a walking contradiction.

Was that happening to me? My daughter was beginning to reject much of what Laurine and I had taught her. Had I failed as a father? Only later would I come to see that she was just growing up. She was owning and personalizing her faith as an adolescent. But the concern was real. I felt the words mockingly shouted at Jesus, "Physician, heal thyself!" I was trapped in a near clinical depression. I had bottomed out.

Not only had I picked up the old shoe of compulsive overeating, but I had begun to drink too much. My friends saw only this symptom of collapse and rushed in with the solution that I voluntarily enter an institution for alcoholics. As you can imagine, at the bottom of the pit, their suggestion filled me with fear.

Fortunately, by the grace of God I was able to surrender my life to God and seek his help out of that pit. Through following the Twelve Steps, I learned that I did not suffer from alcoholism, but from compulsive overeating and other codependent patterns. I entered counseling—a relationship that I never thought would be beneficial to me.

As I re-examined my entire life, scales fell from my eyes and I saw the influence of my past and the mistakes of my present. I saw that even my religious faith had become compulsive. It, in and of itself, was starting to operate as a substance in my life. I found that no person except myself was telling me I had to live the exacting, burdensome life I had embarked upon in the name of God.

Yes, a system I had helped build at home, at work, and in ministry was adding to my burden. But behind this system was a compulsion, a drive from deep within me. I was seeking to fill the hole in my soul and prove I was worth something. Prove to whom? Prove to God, my wife, and others. But I had failed! And I had nowhere to go but the bottom of the pit. There I found the truth of the words that Betsie Ten Boom had spoken to her sister, Corrie: "No pit is too deep that God isn't deeper still." I discovered my own powerlessness and utter need for God.

So even a wrongful intervention became an occasion of grace. A personal collapse and fall became an opportunity for a deeper conversion. As C.S. Lewis so wonderfully expressed it, "The cross comes before the crown." God reached down into my pit and used my pain, failure, brokenness, and hurt to get to a deeper place in my heart and then began filling my hole within. Like Thomas Merton, "God alone" became my motto.

I am happy to report that the process begun in that long-ago conversion continues one day at a time. I am still in recovery. But my perspective has changed. I have come to understand that recovery must be a lifestyle of continual conversion.

Many things, like compulsive overeating, that I used to think of as sin were, in fact, the bad fruit of codependency. Codependency rooted, yes, in my upbringing—but codependency that was fueled even by my experience on the job and in lay ministry. I am experiencing spiritual freedom from a misunderstanding of myself and my identity in Christ. As St. Paul told the Corinthian Christians, "If anyone is in Christ, he is a new creation" (2 Cor 5:17).

So the layers of chocolate that used to cover this hollow bunny have been stripped away. To use another analogy, think of an onion. As the layers are being peeled away, the process produces tears. But I know that the one who is peeling away my exterior has had only the most loving thing in mind. He is getting to my core. There he is building a throne for himself. I will only experience the complete filling of this hole on the other side of the tomb. That is true for all of us.

In the meantime, the one whose voice of command will open our tombs on the last day is revealing to me his heavenly wisdom.

Of this wisdom St. Paul writes:

We do, however, speak a message of wisdom among the mature, but not the wisdom of this age or of the rulers of this age, who are coming to nothing. No, we speak of God's secret wisdom, a wisdom that has been hidden and that God destined for our glory before time began. None of the rulers of this age understood it, for if they had, they would not have crucified the Lord of glory. However, as it is written: "No eye has seen, no ear has heard, no mind has conceived what God has prepared for those who love him" but God has revealed it to us by his Spirit. The Spirit searches all things, even the deep things of God. 1 Cor 2:6-10, NIV

While the Christian life is often one of suffering and struggle, it also can be a life of recovery and renewal. Its purpose is our transformation into the likeness of God and its final goal is eternity with him. Rather than a pious dream, this vision is a source of "unspeakable joy." It is a wonderful privilege to be called children of God! The beloved disciple John reminds us: "Beloved, we are God's children now; what we will be has not yet been revealed. What we do know is this: when he is revealed, we will be like him, for we will see him as he is. And all who have this hope in him purify themselves, just as he is pure" (1 Jn 3:2-3).

God is at work in me. He is at work in you. He is purifying and preparing us for eternity. Purification involves fire. That fire for most of us is the struggle of our daily lives. For some like me, the discovery of my codependency has been a lifeline to recovery—a road I never want to leave. I have found that the life of recovery is truly that of a disciple of the one who proclaimed himself, "the way, the truth, and the life." This hollow bunny is on that road, and each step draws me closer to completion, my perfection in Christ.

I am finally comfortable with my nakedness, because I know that God sees all things. It is interesting that in Genesis, after the fall of the first man and woman, the Lord called to them, "Where are you?" And Adam answered, "I heard the sound of you in the garden, and I was afraid, because I was naked; and I hid myself." And he said, "Who told you that you were naked? Have you eaten from the tree of which I commanded you not to eat?" (Gn 3:9-11).

The immediate result of their rebellion was a sense of shame because they were exposed. This was the beginning of toxic shame. As I find myself experiencing liberation from toxic shame, I am comfortable with who I am. I accept that I am a work-in-process, that God is not finished with me yet. As God gives me understanding, I will seek to minimize my predominant faults.

I hope that there will be no more layers of chocolate or pretense, no more false clothing of pride and willfulness, no more proud self-sufficiency. I hope that I will no longer confuse the kissing cousins of codependency and sin. At moments of weakness, though, I still flirt with denial, the illusion of control, and avoidance. But for me, one day at a time, just as I am, I want to follow after him. I look ahead with a hope that will not disappoint. Finally, I can look back with new glasses and see that even when I fell, he was there to pick me up. Even the pain of my falling became his instrument of healing. After all, he is love, and "love never fails" (1 Cor 13:8, NIV).

In the words of St. Paul: "When I was a child, I spoke like a child, I thought like a child, I reasoned like a child; when I became an adult, I put an end to childish ways. For now we see in a mirror, dimly, but then we shall see face to face. Now I know only in part; then I will know fully, even as I have been fully known" (1 Cor 13:11-13).

Looking back, I see God's marvelous handiwork. At times I

have just seen the outside edges or the messy threads on the back of this intricate and beautiful design. But one day I know I will see the whole beautiful tapestry of my life. Each of our lives is a tapestry designed by the author of life. In the next chapter, I will give you a glimpse of that tapestry in my life, so put on your new glasses and be prepared to see afresh with the eyes of faith.

CHAPTER 11 | The Beautiful Tapestry of Our Lives

For it was you who formed my inward parts; you knit me together in my mother's womb. I praise you, for I am fearfully and wonderfully made. Wonderful are your works; that I know very well.

Ps 139:13-14

YOU AND I ARE WONDERFULLY MADE. God knew what he was doing when he created us. And now he is weaving a beautiful tapestry in each of our lives. My move to Virginia has taught me something about that reality and the pace of life in general.

Things move slower in the South. Yet that doesn't mean less is accomplished. Southerners have simply discovered one of the great secrets of life. All of our fretting, worrying, and fast-paced approach to life can often leave us running in place. We become like dogs chasing after our own tails and running in circles.

Southerners know how to set a measured, dignified pace to daily life, something I can appreciate the need for as a transplanted Bostonian. There's a certain grandeur and even a folksy sort of wisdom that one picks up down South.

RECOGNIZING AND APPRECIATING GOD'S MASTER PLAN

One folksy anecdote was shared by a friend who grew up in Alabama. He described with fondness being taken to his grandmother and mother's weaving and quilting bees in the summer. His mother and grandmother would join other weavers and quilters on a summer afternoon, setting up their looms and other supplies in a grassy field with plenty of shade trees.

He recalls crawling under a row of weaving looms and seeing strand after strand of thread hanging down in a confused jumble of colors and lines. A curious toddler, he would crawl through the back side of a row of looms until he found his way out. One day he was finally big enough to reach his little arms around and grab ahold of the front side of a loom. Ever so slowly, he lifted himself up and beheld the majesty of an intricate tapestry. What had looked for so long from the ground and the back side of the looms like a confused mish-mash of color and line was a beautiful, breathtaking design that was being completed by some weavers.

That experience deeply affected my friend. He grew up and went on to become a dynamic Baptist minister. He uses this story regularly to illustrate the sovereignty of God and his master plan for each of our lives. "You see," he says, "God is at work in each of our lives, weaving a tapestry the beauty of which we will only perceive when we are with him, looking down. Every now and then," he continues, "we can get a grasp of the design, but most of our lives we see only the strands."

Faith tells us that the one who ordered the universe, who created humanity from dust and who set the stars in their place, is at work in each of our lives. But only as we grow older, do we usually begin to see the pattern of God's purpose and design with some clarity.

As we catch glimpses of God's design for our lives, a fundamental truth is that all of us are needy. The sooner and more often we admit it to ourselves and God, the sooner he can answer our needs. In remembering just how needy I am, I experience how sufficient and powerful God really is.

THE CHALLENGE OF HUMILITY AND LOVE

The choice we continually face is between self-sufficiency and reliance on God alone. The choice is between powerlessness and pretense. The following story Jesus told illustrates this imperative:

> To some who are confident of their own righteousness and look down on everybody else, Jesus told this parable: "Two men went up to the temple to pray, one a Pharisee and the other a tax collector. The Pharisee stood up and prayed *about* himself. 'God, I thank you that I am not like all other men—robbers, evildoers, adulterers—or even like this tax collector. I fast twice a week and give a tenth of all I get.' But the tax collector stood at a distance. He would not even look up to heaven, but beat his breast and said, 'God, have mercy on me, a sinner.' I tell you that this man, rather than the other, went home justified before God.
>
> **Lk 18:9-14, NIV, emphasis mine**

One of my greatest problems in my struggle with codependency has been understanding biblical humility. I have been confused too about what Scripture means by self-denial. Why? Because of my own poor self-image. Only in the past six years have I gained a healthy concept of self-love. Love of God, neighbor, and self creates balance in our lives.

Jesus' story about the Pharisee and tax collector helps me understand how these three loves relate. In praying only about himself and praising what he had done, the Pharisee denigrated God and others. But the tax collector understood his utter need for God's mercy and love. He went home justified. Love, after all, is the "fulfillment of the law." God himself is love. He loves us and is always interested in our good. He knows what is good for us far better than we do, and he knows how to bring it about in his time and in his way. Hear the words of the beloved disciple John:

> So we have known and believe the love that God has for us. God is love, and those who abide in love abide in God, and God abides in them. Love has been perfected among us in this: that we may have boldness on the day of judgment, because he is, so are we in this world. There is no fear in love, but perfect love casts out fear, for fear has to do with punishment, and whoever fears has not reached perfection in love. We love because he first loved us. Those who say, "I love God," and hate their brothers or sisters, are liars; for those who do not love a brother or sister, whom they have seen, cannot love God, whom they have not seen. The commandment we have from him is this: those who love God must love their brothers and sisters also.   1 Jn 4:16-21

The ultimate goal of God's beautiful design is to perfect his love in us. After all, love is the highest virtue. We contemporary Christians all too often forget that.

Reflecting on this tendency to forget the importance of love, C.S. Lewis wrote:

> If you asked twenty good men today what they thought the highest of the virtues, nineteen of them would reply, Unselfishness. But if you had asked almost any of the great Christians of old, he would have replied, Love. You see what has happened? A negative term has been substituted for a positive, and this is of more than philological importance. The negative idea of Unselfishness carries with it the suggestion not primarily of securing good things for others, but of

going without them ourselves, as if our abstinence and not their happiness was the important point. I do not think this is the Christian virtue of Love. The New Testament has lots to say about self-denial, but not about self-denial as an end in itself. We are told to deny ourselves and to take up our crosses in order that we may follow Christ; and to nearly every description of what we shall ultimately find if we do so contains an appeal to desire. If there lurks in most modern minds the notion that to desire our own good and earnestly to hope for the enjoyment of it is a bad thing, I submit that this notion has crept in from Kant and the Stoics and is no part of the Christian faith. Indeed, if we consider the unblushing promises of reward and the staggering nature of the rewards promised in the Gospels, it would seem that Our Lord finds our desires not too strong, but too weak. We are half-hearted creatures, fooling about with drink and sex and ambition when infinite joy is offered us, like an ignorant child who wants to go on making mud pies in a slum because he cannot imagine what is meant by the offer of a holiday at the sea. We are far too easily pleased. We must not be troubled by unbelievers when they say that this promise of reward makes the Christian life a mercenary affair.[1]

The self-denial demonstrated by the tax collector in the parable taught by Jesus is not self-hatred or low self-esteem, but an honest acknowledgment of his utter need—an admission of his powerlessness to change without the love and mercy of God. He wanted the best for himself, which is God's love. The New Testament calls us to self-denial, but not as an end in itself. It is, rather, an essential element in developing a life of love, a way of being transformed into love.

If our yearning for God leads us to Calvary, instead of to self-made mountains which we try to climb on our own power, we will discover love is a free gift and not something we can earn. We need to let our difficulties teach us how to love as Jesus loved.

We see this kind of love etched in the face of a Mother Teresa or a Fr. Philip Bebie. We have been created for such love. It is what we will spend eternity doing—loving and being loved. Even what appears to be tragedy, like the death of my friend Fr. Philip, is a vehicle for God's love being manifested. Look at how Philip's life touched mine. I hope it has touched yours. Through the ages, the lives and deaths of men and women who have truly loved have borne fruit in countless ways.

Though we are a product of our past, we are not chained to it. Instead, we are rooted in what good can be derived from it. Good is defined by the one who is all good, and he is at work in us. All he asks for is our love.

GOD MEETS US AT OUR DEEPEST POINT OF NEED

One of the most wonderful stories in the New Testament is the story of the Samaritan woman:

A Samaritan woman came to draw water, and Jesus said to her, "Give me a drink." (His disciples had gone to the city to buy food.) The Samaritan woman said to him, "How is it that you, a Jew, ask a drink of me, a woman of Samaria?" (Jews do not share things in common with Samaritans.) Jesus answered her, "If you knew the gift of God, and who it is that is saying to you, 'Give me a drink,' you would have asked him, and he would have given you living water." The woman said to him, "Sir, you have no bucket, and the well is deep. Where do you get that living water? Are you greater than our ancestor Jacob, who gave us the well, and with his sons and his flocks drank from it?" Jesus said to her, "Everyone who drinks of this water will be thirsty again, but those who drink of the water that I will give them will never be thirsty. The water that I will give will become in them a spring of water gushing up to eternal life." The woman said to him, "Sir, give me this water, so that I may never be thirsty or have to keep coming here to draw water."

Jesus said to her, "Go, call your husband, and come back." The woman answered him, "I have no husband." Jesus said to her, "You are right in saying, 'I have no husband'; for you have had five husbands, and the one you have now is not your husband. What you have said is true!" The woman said to him, "Sir, I see that you are a prophet." **Jn 4: 7-19**

Jesus encounters us just as he did the Samaritan woman. He knew the woman before they even met. He knew what she was made of, and he saw right through her to the heart of her predicament. He understood her pain and met her at her point of deepest need. So he is with us. We can hide nothing from Jesus. In our relationship with him, "... whatever is hidden is meant to be disclosed, and whatever is concealed is meant to be brought out into the open" (Mk 4:22, NIV).

The Twelve Steps have been a tremendous opportunity for opening up my life to God and others who love me. This has become possible, however, only through authentic self-acceptance and self-love. I am only beginning to grasp true biblical humility. For years I mouthed an understanding of biblical humility—that it was taking the position of a servant, of a "lesser." However, I had never understood the deeper reality that in Jesus Christ, we, his disciples, are really no longer servants. Hear his wonderful words:

"This is my commandment, that you love one another as I have loved you. No one has greater love than this, to lay down one's life for one's friends. You are my friends if you do what I command you. I do not call you servants any longer, because the servant does not know what the master is doing; but I have called you friends, because I have made known to you everything that I have heard from my Father. You did not choose me but I chose you. And I appointed you to go and bear fruit, fruit that will last, so that the Father

will give you whatever you ask him in my name. I am giving
you these commands so that you may love one another."

Jn 15:12-17

In the same chapter, Jesus teaches the disciples about pruning, telling them that he is the "true vine" and his Father is the
"gardener." That lesson explains how critical it is that we stay in
a close relationship with him and that our relationship with
him involves pruning.

Recently we had to have some tree work done in our front
yard in Chesapeake, Virginia. A tree surgeon came to remove
some dead branches on a beautiful oak tree in the yard. I was
not prepared for the tree surgeon's diagnosis. "Well," he said,
"you need to lop off this entire portion of the tree." That was
nearly half of the tree! After he explained why to me, I agreed
for him to proceed. He was right. The tree is now flourishing.

Pruning is painful. Jesus tells us that the Father "... removes
every branch in me that bears no fruit. Every branch that bears
fruit he prunes to make it bear more fruit" (Jn 15:2). Pruning
produces fruitfulness in each of our lives.

We cannot fool God, so why not be candid with him? For
many of us who have struggled with codependency, compulsions, or addictions, this is not easy to do. Perhaps when we
have been honest with others, we have been deeply hurt or
even abused. Perhaps such abuse has happened more times
than we care to count. But it is against God's nature to abuse.
He is perfect love.

Jesus told the Samaritan woman to go call her husband. She
honestly responded, "I have no husband." Jesus, seeing her
heart, told her that he knew that from the beginning. He knew
that she had, in fact, five husbands and that she was at that
moment involved in an illicit relationship. Seems judgmental
at first, doesn't it? But it was his uncompromising honesty with
the Samaritan woman that revealed to her the depths of his
love. He met her at her deepest, most vulnerable point of
need. There in the midst of the pain, the shame, and the sin,

he unconditionally loved her, as he beheld the beautiful tapestry he would weave of her life.

She, in turn, did not hide her past, but openly revealed it. She became a believer because Jesus gave her eyes to see: "The woman said to him, 'I know that Messiah is coming (who is called Christ). When he comes, he will explain all things to us.' Jesus said to her, 'I am he, the one who is speaking to you'" (Jn 4:25-26).

What a wonderful encounter and what a wonderful gift! Jesus gave this woman a gift of new glasses. He also gave her the gift of eternal life. To many who thought themselves righteous, God's truth was hidden, but not from this humble Samaritan woman who had been honest with Jesus.

Once in Jesus' travels through the countryside, he wept over the cities he passed. Why? Because the people in them did not have the honesty and humility to repent. They had failed to be honest about their own need of God and relied on their own self-righteousness. After his stinging rebuke of the unrepentant cities, he stopped to pray:

> "I praise you, Father, Lord of heaven and earth, because you have hidden these things from the wise and learned, and revealed them to little children. Yes, Father, for this was your good pleasure.
>
> "All things have been committed to me by my Father. No one knows the Son except the Father, and no one knows the Father except the Son and those to whom the Son chooses to reveal him.
>
> "Come to me, all you who are weary and burdened, and I will give you rest. Take my yoke upon you and learn from me, for I am gentle and humble in heart, and you will find rest for your souls. For my yoke is easy and my burden is light. Mt. 11:25-30, NIV

Isn't it incredible that these things are "hidden" from the "wise and learned" and revealed to "little children"? What is it that Jesus is trying to tell us? Certainly not that we are to be childish. Rather, that we are to be completely honest and humble about who we are and about our need for God and others. This is what set the Samaritan woman free.

The Samaritan woman is a model for each of us as we go to the well of the waters of life. We need hide nothing. God knows it all, already. When we surrender ourselves to him, he can take even what we fear and transform it. Out of the ashes of our past, he can weave an intricate tapestry more glorious than we could ever imagine.

As a teenager in the late 1960s, I attended a concert of one of my favorite performers, James Taylor. Unbeknownst to the crowd, James Taylor decided to introduce Carole King that evening. Perhaps you are of my generation and remember Carole King, who was to become famous. That evening she sang a song called "Tapestry," which describes how our lives are like a beautiful tapestry that we only catch glimpses of in this life.

So it has been with my life. Years later I reflect on the message of that song. God is indeed weaving a beautiful tapestry of my life, even though I can only catch glimpses of the work-in-process on his loom. From that perspective, I can honestly say I would not now change a thing, even the most painful wounds in my life because they have all been beautifully used by him to create the pattern that is my life.

As I shared earlier, it was tough breaking into law school and connecting with the material, both because of the intense workload and the use of the Socratic dialogue in class. Professor Brown, who taught property law at my law school, took his assignment especially seriously. He was constantly firing off questions at his befuddled students. No matter how hard some of us shrank in our chairs to avoid his glares, it was not possible. Fear of that class grew in all of us students.

Perhaps the worst experience came one Thursday afternoon when, after not receiving the correct answer from a student, Professor Brown retorted, "I hope that I am not called in to testify before the Bar Association at your disbarment, counselor." All the class was shocked, and the student felt shamed. Later in the class, Professor Brown did apologize to the student, "Counselor, I was a little rough on you. However, wouldn't you rather it be me than your client? Remember, your client will depend upon your legal skills for his or her life. It is my job as a law professor to teach you to do your best for your client."

It is ironic that today I regard his class as the finest I ever had. You see, Professor Brown made us think like lawyers, even though his class was difficult.

If you are anything like me, you tend to avoid most difficult things. But they often produce the best results. In the tapestry of our lives, God is weaving his beautiful plan. When we surrender ourselves to him and acknowledge our own powerlessness, he can take even what we fear and transform it.

With that tapestry in view, Lord Jesus, I am grateful for the family that I was raised in, warts and all. For without my childhood experiences, I would not be who I am today. I would not have experienced your wonderful grace as the unmerited favor of my Savior at my deepest point of need.

Lord, I am grateful for the failures and struggles because each time I fell, I was able to see your purpose more clearly. Each time I fell, I was able to put aside my futile efforts at control, denial, and avoidance. I began to realize I could not render a perfect performance and had to surrender my "hurdle mentality" to you. Lord, I am grateful even for the trauma of that intervention on that cold afternoon in March. That painful event forced me to begin to deal with my codependency. Lord, that process of recovery has been for me a new lease on life—a new conversion of sorts.

Through it all, Lord, I have come to understand the gospel even more profoundly than I did before. I have come to understand the call to perfection as the completion of God's work in me—a project that will last a lifetime. I see now that I need to wait patiently for that completion in Christ. I have come to understand your love even more profoundly than I did before.

Lord, you took what was wrong and intended for harm and turned it to good. All things do indeed "... work together for good for those who love [you]" (Rom 8:28).

Lord Jesus, through the pain, the suffering, and the struggle of being overweight, impatient, and intolerant—even in my struggles with sin—you have woven a beautiful tapestry of my life. Through my daily dying, hopes, fears, hurts, diets, exercise programs, continuing conversion, powerlessness, growth in faith, and even disappointments—you continue to weave a beautiful tapestry of my life. For that I am eternally grateful, Lord. Amen.

Conclusion

WE BEGAN OUR JOURNEY together with a tribute to Fr. Philip and now we come back to him. His life and death speak volumes about love—the love of God and our love for God. In great pain and a decaying body, Fr. Philip told me, "God is good." He was right. Cancer is not good, nor is pain intrinsically good, but God is good. And in his goodness, he can fashion a way of recovery and renewal out of our suffering and struggle.

Fr. Philip has been healed. Why do I say that? Because for every believer, death is the ultimate healing. It is also the great equalizer. No human escapes it. But on the other side of death, is life eternal. Fr. Philip has received his heavenly reward. With eyes fixed on the eternal, he embraced his earthly life with all of its imperfections.

Through Fr. Philip's example and the great mercy of God, I am learning the mystery of suffering that leads to death and glory. Like all the saints, we experience pain. The key is how we handle it. The choices we make often affect whether we see the hand and glory of God in the midst of it.

A man who I greatly admire is a seventy-five-year-young Baptist pastor in Alabama. He has the kind of wisdom that one only garners from age, struggle, and wounds that heal.

When I first met this pastor he shared with me about the wounds that he had experienced in his life. Yet he concluded by talking about the wonderful mercy and love God had manifested in them and through them.

This godly man shared with me about a particulary traumatic collapse in ministry. He looked me straight in the eye after sharing with absolute candor about his weakness and said, "Son, it was then that I learned to stop seeking the hand of the Lord and start seeking his face. For sixty-three years I had sought a hand-out from God. Yet, the psalmist says '"Come," my heart says, "seek his face!" Your face, Lord, do I seek' (Ps 27:8). It was only when I fell all the way down and looked up that I finally understood what he meant. To seek his face means to look into his eyes and be transformed by his love. To seek his face means to seek his sovereign leadership in my life no matter what. To seek his face means to be more concerned with loving than receiving." He concluded, "Son, if I could give you any advice, stop seeking his hand and seek his face." In some instances, for this pastor and for me, the wounds have completely healed. In other cases, for both of us, the wounds are still healing.

This was the kind of advice that Fr. Philip gave me. It seems to seep in a little at a time.

I am beginning to think very differently about this whole subject of wounds that heal and the role of suffering and struggle in a life of recovery and renewal. For me, I have found that recovery and renewal go hand in hand. The ultimate goal of a Twelve-Step recovery process for a Christian is transformation into the image of Jesus. That is also the ultimate goal of renewal and conversion. The life of faith and the process of recovery can, and should, lead down the same road.

The Twelve Steps and the Christian life, rather than being in competition, can be complementary. In fact, if we really understand the nature of conversion and recovery, we discover that they can be fundamentally the same reality for Christians. At the beginning of both journeys, we acknowledge our powerlessness and willingly surrender our lives to God. Along the way, we acknowledge our problems and our sin. We take responsibility for our lives, while remembering who is really in control.

If you take anything away from this book at all, take that sense of surrender. Give up. Let go and let God. He never promised to make the pain go away, but to make you look like Jesus.

In my life, I am coming to love my wounds. I am certainly not a masochist. However, I have seen that my weakness and struggle has brought me closer to the foot of the cross of the one who transforms my weakness by his love. I wonder what I'll look like in my resurrected body. Will my glorified body bear my wounds, as does the Master's? Will your glorified body as well? If so, by then we will see those wounds as beautiful and glorious marks of love. Why? Because they will have healed and transformed us. Or rather God will have healed us through them. It is in that sense that Philip has been healed.

He is in great company now—the company of that great "cloud of witnesses" (Heb 12:1), the company of the saints, martyrs, and champions of love. He, and they, "having finished the race" urge us on to our goal. They are in the presence of Jesus, who ran the race before them, leaving an example: "... looking to Jesus the pioneer and perfecter of our faith, who for the sake of the joy that was set before him endured the cross, disregarding its shame, and has taken his seat at the right hand of the throne of God. Consider him who endured such hostility against himself from sinners, so that you may not grow weary or lose heart" (Heb 12:2-3).

They now await final completion, the resurrection of their bodies. What a marvelous truth of the Christian faith! So powerful is the transforming love of God that it will completely renew our bodies and, indeed, the whole temporal order.

A foreshadowing of this great event, the hope of all Christians, is set forth in an intriguing passage in St. Matthew's Gospel:

> Then Jesus cried again with a loud voice and breathed his last. At that moment the curtain of the temple was torn in

two, from top to bottom. The earth shook, and the rocks were split. The tombs also were opened, and many bodies of the saints who had fallen asleep [had died] were raised. After his resurrection they came out of the tombs and entered the holy city and appeared to many. Now when the centurion and those with him, who were keeping watch over Jesus, saw the earthquake and what took place, they were terrified and said, "Truly this man was God's Son!" **Mt 27:50-54**

One day we all will come out of our tombs. We will experience a new heaven and a new earth. I want to walk again then with my friend Fr. Philip and thank him for his life and his death.

In the final book of the Bible, Revelation, we are given a glimpse of what awaits us:

Then I saw a new heaven and a new earth; for the first heaven and the first earth had passed away, and the sea was no more. And I saw the holy city, the new Jerusalem, coming down out of heaven from God, prepared as a bride adorned for her husband. And I heard a loud voice from the throne saying, "See, the home of God is among mortals. He will dwell with them as their God; they will be his peoples, and God himself will be with them; he will wipe every tear from their eyes. Death will be no more, mourning and crying and pain will be no more, for the first things have passed away." And the one who was seated on the throne said, "See, I am making all things new!" Also he said, "Write this, for these words are trustworthy and true." **Rv 21:1-5**

God *will* make all things new and bring an end to pain someday. Between now and then, we are called to live to the fullest, faithful to the one who has shown us the way, to embrace each day as a gift from God, and to persevere through the pain and struggle that are part of this earthly city.

I still have the ornamental tree Fr. Philip gave me. It stands on my mantle as a symbol of the tree of life which will be present in the kingdom to come:

> Then the angel showed me the river of the water of life, bright as crystal, flowing from the throne of God and of the Lamb through the middle of the street of the city. On either side of the river is the tree of life with its twelve kinds of fruit, producing its fruit each month; and the leaves of the tree are for the healing of the nations. Nothing accursed will be found there any more. But the throne of God and of the Lamb will be in it and his servants will worship him; they will see his face, and his name will be on their foreheads. And there will be no more night; they need no light of lamp or sun, for the Lord God will be their light, and they will reign forever and ever. Rv 22:1-5

The leaves of that tree on my mantle are a tribute to the one who taught me what true healing is all about. Every time I forget this reality, I consider again the example of Fr. Philip. After all, he is waiting for me on the inside.

Notes

ONE
Tribute to Fr. Philip

1. Now called *Franciscan University of Steubenville*, the university is a tribute to what a Catholic school can be if it chooses to be openly and unapologetically Catholic and Christian. Its story is told in *Let the Fire Fall*, Michael Scanlan, T.O.R., (Ann Arbor, MI: Servant Publications, 1986) and in *Evangelical Catholics*, Keith A. Fournier (Nashville, TN: Thomas Nelson Publishers, 1991).

TWO
Denial—One of the Games We Play

1. Details of my search for the truth as a teenager, which eventually brought me to the foot of the cross and returned me to the heart of my Catholic faith, can be found in *Evangelical Catholics*, Fournier, 28-33.
2. Recently on the Christian market there have appeared sensationalist books opposing the Twelve-Step process. It is, in my opinion, an unfortunate and largely misinformed overreaction. Similarly, even the secular media has been trumpeting the issue. See, for example the February 17, 1992 Issue of *Newsweek* magazine, "The Curse of Self-Esteem." Some popular Christian periodicals have sought to present a balanced discussion of the issue. See, for example, "Christian Psychotherapy: Can It Help the Problem of Sin?" in the March 1992 issue of *Charisma* magazine.
3. John Bradshaw, *Healing the Shame that Binds You* (Deerfield Beach, FL: Health Communications, Inc., 1988), vii.
4. See for example, *Toxic Faith* by Stephen Arterburn and Jack Felton (Nashville, TN: Thomas Nelson Publishers, 1991). Also see *Churches That Abuse* by Ronald M. Enroth (Grand Rapids, MI: Zondervan Book Publishers, 1992).

5. Much of this discussion on Peter as a model for overcoming denial is based on a sermon preached by a dear friend, Pastor Ken Wilson. It and other insightful work is contained in *Recovering a Sincere and Pure Devotion to Christ,* Ken Wilson (Ann Arbor, MI: Emmaus Fellowship, 1992). For this work, write: Emmaus Fellowship, P.O. Box 3517, Ann Arbor, MI 48106.

THREE
The Grand Illusion of Control

1. Martin Anderson, *Revolution* (San Diego, CA: Harcourt, Brace, Jovanovich, 1988), 315-316.
2. Anderson, *Revolution,* 316.
3. The matter of the interior motivation for compulsive overeating has been dealt with extensively. See, for example, *You Can't Quit until You Know What's Eating You: Overcoming Compulsive Overeating,* Donna LaBlanc, M.Ed., L.P.C. (Deerfield Beach, FL: Health Communications, Inc., 1990), M. Billich, *Weight Loss from the Inside Out: Help for the Compulsive Eater,* (San Francisco, CA: Harper & Row, 1983).
4. John and Linda Friel, *Adult Children: The Secrets of Dysfunctional Families* (Deerfield Beach, FL: Health Communications, Inc., 1988), 26-27.
5. John Bradshaw, *Bradshaw on: The Family* (Deerfield Beach, FL: Health Communications, Inc., 1988), 80.
6. See for example, *The Subtle Danger of Spiritual Abuse,* by David Johnson and Jeff van Vonderen (Minneapolis, MN: Bethany House Publishers, 1991). For an excellent discussion of family as a system, see John Bradshaw's *Bradshaw on: The Family* (Deerfield Beach, FL: Health Communications, Inc. 1988) and John and Linda Friel's *Adult Children: The Secrets of Dysfunctional Families* (Deerfield Beach, FL: Health Communications, Inc., 1988).
7. Many groups of all sorts have become aware of the operation of control and denial among both their leaders and members. They have realized the importance of healthy, honest admission as the first step toward recovery. Such groups have sought pastoral assistance from the broader church and have shown tremendous courage in reforming and restructuring their organizations.
8. Melody Beattie, *Codependents' Guide to the Twelve Steps* (New York, NY: Prentice Hall Press, 1990), 23-24.
9. "Evangelical moments" is a concept that I introduced in *Evangelical Catholics* to refer to those moments of conversion in a Christian's life when he or she is attempting to walk in the light and follow the Lord daily. Such a walk with the Lord must be daily. Yesterday's honesty and surrender will not cover today or tomorrow's concerns.

10. In *Evangelical Catholics*, I even adapted the Twelve Steps as a vehicle for healing the rifts in the whole body of Christ arguing that, no matter how real our doctrinal differences are, much of what separates us is relational and inherited. We are children of the great divorce that besieged the whole Christian people centuries ago.

11. Codependency is a developing concept. The word used to refer specifically to those who were affected directly by an addicted spouse. However, it has become increasingly clear that the family itself is a system. Addictions and dysfunctions affect many more people. A good working definition is taken from *Love Is a Choice* by Robert Hemfelt, Frank Minirth, and Paul Meier (Nashville, TN: Thomas Nelson Publishers, 1989). In the book, *Love Is a Choice*, the authors define codependency as an addiction to people (by assuming the role of rescuer or victim), behaviorial problems (such as workaholism, anger, sexual acting out, and perfectionism), and things that control and obsess us (including alcohol and drugs, money, and food). Codependency arises from the fallacy of trying to control inner feelings by manipulating other people and circumstances.

    The following ten points can identify a codependent:

    1. driven by one or more compulsions;
    2. bound and tormented by the way things were in the dysfunctional family of origin;
    3. self-esteem (and often maturity) is very low;
    4. certain his or her happiness hinges on others;
    5. conversely, feels inordinately responsible for others;
    6. relationship with a spouse or Significant Other Person (SOP) is marred by a damaging, unstable lack of balance between dependence and independence;
    7. a master of denial and repression;
    8. worries about things he or she can't change and may well try to change them;
    9. life is punctuated by extremes;
    10. continually looking for the something that is lacking or missing in life.

    Any addiction, including codependent addiction, will ultimately take its toll on our lives, because an addict will do anything, or give up anything, to satisfy his or her addiction. Frustration and misery are the results.

12. "Family of origin" refers to your natural or adoptive family. In other words, it is the family in which you were reared. Your "family of affiliation" in recovery literature refers to the group (whether it be a Twelve-Step group or a church group) in which you have chosen to work through the implications of what occurred in your family of origin.

13. "Adult child" refers to adults, such as myself and countless others, who have not completely resolved the detrimental influences that shaped them while growing up in a dysfunctional family. Something in the normal maturation process was stunted, and healing and growth are needed. As a result, such individuals are still affected as adults by the events of their childhood. Adult children typically go through a process of "reparenting." Reparenting refers to the process of reviewing your own childhood with a view toward making up for the deficiencies in your own background. In other words, you, in a sense, now become your own parent and allow your "inner child" the freedom to feel, grow, hurt, and become what you as a child were prevented from feeling and becoming because of a dysfunctional family background. This is similar to what years ago came to be called in Christian renewal circles "inner healing." Both processes have a similar goal—wholeness, completion, and freedom. But there is an important difference. For the Christian, inner healing is accomplished by the healing power of Christ and not primarily by becoming your own parent. All healing ultimately comes from God and *not* from ourselves.

14. "Higher power" is used in most Twelve-Step programs to refer to God. Though some new Twelve-Step programs seek to delete it and avoid religion altogether, such an approach is misguided and will fail miserably. Without God, no full and complete recovery is possible.

FOUR
Avoidance—It Just Makes Things Worse

1. "Recovery Community" is used by those who have in any way been touched by the Twelve-Step movement. It refers to a general group of people who have realized that they have been detrimentally affected by dysfunctional family life, codependency, substance abuse (sometimes even spiritual abuse), or abuse of any sort. In handling such issues, these people have found freedom and assistance through various Twelve-Step programs. Most of these programs owe their origin to the original Twelve Steps of Alcoholics Anonymous. However, these steps have been developed and adapted for use in overcoming many other areas of personal addiction, compulsion, codependency, or abuse.

2. Bishop Fulton John Sheen, *Treasure in Clay: The Autobiography of Fulton J. Sheen* (Garden City, NY: Doubleday, 1980), 334.

3. For the full story of my faith journey, see *Evangelical Catholics* by Keith A. Fournier, (Nashville, TN: Thomas Nelson Publishers, 1991). Also see, Keith A. Fournier, *Bringing Christ's Presence Into Your Home: Your Family as a Domestic Church* (Nashville, TN: Thomas Nelson Publishers, 1992).

4. From a sermon by St. Leo the Great, pope (Sermon 15, *De Passione*

Domini, 3-4: PL 54, 366-367), *The Liturgy of the Hours,* Vol. II (New York, NY: Catholic Book Publishing Company, 1976).

FIVE
Predominant Faults—Our Self-Destruction or
Clay in the Master's Hands?

1. John and Linda Friel, *Adult Children: The Secrets of Dysfunctional Families* (Deerfield Beach, FL: Health Communications, Inc., 1988).
2. William Barclay, *The Daily Study Bible Series: The Letters of James and Peter* (Philadelphia, PA: Westminster Press, 1975), 60.

SIX
Taking Personal Responsibility

1. For a marvelous treatment on the dynamics of legalism and the freedom of grace see Ken Wilson, *Recovering a Sincere and Pure Devotion to Christ,* (Ann Arbor, MI: Emmaus Fellowship, 1992).
2. Wilson, *Recovering a Sincere and Pure Devotion to Christ,* 26.
3. Wilson, *Recovering a Sincere and Pure Devotion to Christ,* 29.
4. Melody Beattie, *Codependents' Guide to the Twelve Steps* (New York, NY: Prentice Hall Press, 1990), 85.
5. For my experience of the revival at Franciscan University, see chapter four in my book *Evangelical Catholics* (Nashville, TN: Thomas Nelson Publishers, 1990).
6. For a wonderful treatment of the recycling process see Melody Beattie, *Beyond Codependency: And Getting Better All the Time* (Center City, MN: Harper/Hazelden, 1989), 45-75.
7. A wonderful book has been written bearing this name, on the issue of recovery. See Frank Minirth and Paul Meier, *Love Hunger,* (Nashville, TN: Thomas Nelson Publishers, 1989).
8. The apostle Paul tells his young disciple, Timothy, "All scripture is God-breathed and is useful for teaching, rebuking, correcting, and training in righteousness, so that the man of God may be thoroughly equipped for every good work" (2 Tm 3:16). The sacred Scriptures are a fountain of grace in my own personal life and a great gift to all Christians.

SEVEN
The Forgiveness of Sin

1. The wording of Step Five, though similar in all recovery programs is taken specifically from the Twelve Steps for Recovering Codependents.

See Melody Beattie, *Codependents' Guide to the Twelve Steps* (New York, NY: Prentice Hall Press, 1990), 85.

2. Beattie, *Codependents' Guide to the Twelve Steps*, 86-87.

3. Monastic and lay communities alike have been leaders in the ministry of healing since the early 1970s. I lived in a Benedictine community as a religious postulant in the early 1970s.

4. The Second Vatican Council was a landmark in the history of the Roman Catholic Church. Most observers then and now realize that it represented both a major reform and a return to more ancient approaches in catechesis, sacramental life, and theological understandings. For many faithful Catholics of the day, it brought so many changes that it caused serious misunderstandings. However, by the grace of God, the church has survived and blossomed through the sound implementation of the teachings of the Second Vatican Council. Unfortunately, there are those in the church today who seek to cloak their errant doctrine and pastoral practice "in the spirit of Vatican II." However, the spirit they refer to is certainly not that of the council.

5. For an excellent treatment of performance as a vehicle to earning self worth, affirmation, and love, see Robert Hemfelt, Frank Minirth, and Paul Meier, *We Are Driven* (Nashville, TN: Thomas Nelson Publishers, 1991).

6. The account of the fall in Genesis 3 not only shows us original sin, but the pattern of the enemy's attack and our own propensity toward its lure.

7. By the time this book is published, I understand the long awaited bypass through Weirton will be completed.

8. Alan Schreck, *Catholic and Christian* (Ann Arbor, MI: Servant Publications, 1984), 49.

9. *Letter of John Paul II* to All the Priests of the Church on the Occasion of Holy Thursday (Washington, D.C.: United States Catholic Conference), 28-29. For a very helpful treatment of continual conversion and the role of trouble and difficulty in the life of a believer, see Michael Scanlan, T.O.R., *The Truth About Trouble* (Ann Arbor, MI: Servant Publications, 1989).

EIGHT
One Day at a Time

1. *Liturgy of the Hours,* (New York, NY: Catholic Book Publishing Company, 1976) Vol. IV, 425.

2. *Liturgy of the Hours* (New York, NY: Catholic Book Publishing Company, 1976), Vol. II, 555.

3. The revelation of the majesty of God in everyday family life is discussed throughout my book, *Bringing Christ's Presence Into Your Home: Your Family*

as a Domestic Church, (Nashville, TN: Thomas Nelson Publishers, 1992). It is particularly developed in chapters four and five, 50-82.

NINE
Putting on New Glasses—Seeing Anew with the Eyes of Faith

1. Keith A. Fournier, *Evangelical Catholics* (Nashville, TN: Thomas Nelson Publishers, 1990), 100-101.
2. See Keith A. Fournier, *Bringing Christ's Presence Into Your Home: Your Family as a Domestic Church*, chapter eleven, 174.
3. Martin Luther King, Jr., *Strength to Love* (Philadelphia, PA: Fortress Press, 1981), 123-124.
4. King, *Strength to Love*, 95-96.
5. C.S. Lewis, *The Weight of Glory and Other Addresses* (New York, NY: MacMillan Publishing Company, 1980), revised and expanded ed., 18-20.
6. Jim Manney, "Real Power" in *New Covenant* magazine (Ann Arbor, MI: May, 1992), 5.

TEN
Codependency and Sin—Kissing Cousins

1. Alan Schreck, *Basics of the Faith: A Catholic Catechism* (Ann Arbor, MI: Servant Publications, 1987), 217-218.
2. Robert Hemfelt, Frank Minirth, and Paul Meier, *Love Is a Choice: Recovery for Codependent Relationships* (Nashville, TN: Thomas Nelson Publishers, 1989), 11-12. The full text is:

> In its broadest sense, *codependency* can be defined as an *addiction to people, behaviors, or things.* Codependency is the fallacy of trying to control interior feelings by controlling people, things, and events on the outside. To the codependent, control or the lack of it is central to every aspect of life.
>
> The codependent may be addicted to another person. In this interpersonal codependency, the codependent has become so elaborately enmeshed in the other person that the sense of self—personal identity—is severely restricted, crowded out by that other person's identity and problems.
>
> Additionally, codependents can be like *vacuum cleaners gone wild,* drawing to themselves not just another person, but also chemicals (alcohol or drugs, primarily) or things—money, food, sexuality, work. They struggle relentlessly to fill the great emotional vacuum within themselves. Our patients have described it as "walking around feeling like the hole in the center of the doughnut. There is something missing inside me." (emphasis mine)

3. Melody Beattie, *Beyond Codependency: And Getting Better All the Time* (Center City, MN: Harper/Hazelden, 1989), 13.
4. Beattie, *Beyond Codependency,* 14-15.

ELEVEN
The Beautiful Tapestry of Our Lives

1. C.S. Lewis, *The Weight of Glory and Other Addresses* (New York, NY: MacMillan Publishing Co., Inc., 1980), 3-4.